T0197242

EL CONSERVADOR: CONSERVATIVE OPINIONS

EL CONSERVADOR:
CONSERVATIVE
OPINIONS

An American of Mexican Descent Expresses His Views

GEORGE H. RODRIGUEZ

 iUniverse®

EL CONSERVADOR: CONSERVATIVE OPINIONS
AN AMERICAN OF MEXICAN DESCENT EXPRESSES HIS VIEWS

iUniverse books may be ordered through booksellers or by contacting:

iUniverse
1663 Liberty Drive
Bloomington, IN 47403
www.iuniverse.com
1-800-Authors (1-800-288-4677)

Library of Congress Control Number: 2018907778

ISBN: 978-1-5320-5111-1 (sc)
ISBN: 978-1-5320-5112-8 (e)

Print information available on the last page.

iUniverse rev. date: 10/03/2018

Contents

Part 2   Race and Politics

Part 3   Grassroots Politics

Part 4   Liberal Politics and the Media

Introduction

This book is a collection of essays and commentaries written by yours truly, a constitutional conservative Texan of Mexican descent, also known as a Tejano.

The writing reflects my belief in personal freedom and supports the idea that all Texans and Americans should live life as they wish, as long as it does not harm others or infringe on another person's rights.

I believe that personal wealth and personal property ownership are important for the individual pursuit of happiness. Accordingly I also believe in economic freedom, which means that our society should have a free market economy that includes reduced tax rates, reduced government control and regulations, and reduced government spending so all persons have the opportunity to create their own wealth. That means people can earn and keep more money and then develop and grow private businesses so they can hire more people.

I believe that the principles of the US Constitution apply to all governments—local, state, or federal. The Bill of Rights guarantees liberties, protects the rights of citizens, and limits the power of government. However, we must also recognize that the Constitution does not guarantee personal (or collective) success or happiness.

I believe in the constitutional limitations on government. And I believe that all governments (local, state, and federal) should provide only the most basic of public services to citizens and taxpayers while operating within their budgets without deficit spending.

I believe all citizens and taxpayers should be concerned about the $21 trillion federal deficit (as of 2017), plus the state, county, municipal, public school, and other taxing entities' deep debts. Government debt is very dangerous to the freedom and liberty of citizens.

I believe America is the greatest nation on earth with a God-given destiny (if the nation is worthy) and Texas is the greatest state in the nation. I believe in states' rights, which is why the official name of our nation is United States. Therefore I consider myself a citizen of Texas first.

Finally, I believe America and all its states should be cultural melting pots for all people who legally immigrate to our country. I reject "diversity" because I feel it leads to racial, ethnic, and cultural tribalism and divides people. I also reject discrimination, particularly as it is practiced by minorities who disguise it as civil rights and justice.

Accordingly the essays and commentaries in this book are all written from these points of view and in some cases with a little bit of *chile picoso* attitude. I hope you will enjoy them.

George Rodriguez
El Conservador

PART 1
Immigration and Border Security

Amnesty and What It Means to a State like West Virginia

Illegal Immigration

I recently had a conversation with a friend in Charleston, West Virginia, about the immigration-reform debate. As we parted, he mentioned to me that while it was very interesting, he felt that West Virginia residents didn't have a dog in that fight. Unfortunately many people in West Virginia and several other states hold this same view. They feel that the debate over illegal immigration, immigration reform, and amnesty has little to do with them, their communities, and their state. However, the fact is that illegal immigration, immigration reform, and particularly amnesty will have a big impact on West Virginia and other states with low immigrant populations, high unemployment, and a low skilled-labor force.

There is a hot debate in Congress between Republicans and Democrats, liberals and conservatives, about what to do with the eleven million (or more) illegal aliens who already reside in the United States. The popular sentiment is that some type of gradual citizenship should be granted to these persons because deportation would be impossible.

While some of the elected officials don't call it *amnesty*, any type of deferred deportation is a form of amnesty. Whether it is called *amnesty*, *delayed citizenship*, or *legalization with requirements*, the effect and result on West Virginia and other states will be immediate in the form of more federal spending for programs to serve the newcomers.

For instance, the 1986 amnesty had an immediate impact, as it increased the population and poverty levels of certain states. Communities and states that already had large immigrant populations were the most affected directly. But other states were affected indirectly as the federal government created programs for social services.

Furthermore, the 1986 amnesty was supposed to be a onetime-only event, but it has led to the discussion, or demand, of yet another one for an even larger population of illegal aliens. Amnesty rewarded illegal immigration, and it encouraged more of it.

There is another issue for West Virginia and other states with small populations. Federal block grants for housing, health, and other programs are based on the populations and poverty levels of states and communities. Illegal aliens are mostly found in larger states. While West Virginia has had a shrinking population, amnesty will push the state further down the line as other states will increase in population.

Finally, West Virginia's blue-collar workers should understand they will be in direct competition with a new pool of mostly unskilled workers. Whether the jobs are in West Virginia or elsewhere, the national labor and wage competition will affect them.

As someone born and raised in south Texas, I have seen firsthand the impact of labor competition with Mexicans. South Texas border counties are among the poorest in the nation because of uncontrolled immigration (legal and illegal) and the wage and employment competition it creates.

Whatever position West Virginia political leaders take on amnesty and immigration reform, they should understand that amnesty will make an impact on the state. Illegal immigration is illegal, and it should not be rewarded or excused in any form or fashion. Otherwise we only get more illegal immigration.

Deferred Action: Why?

Immigration

Deferred action has always been available to immigrants for special or humanitarian reasons, while law enforcement has always enjoyed so-called prosecutorial discretion. However, we have never seen a deferred-action program systematized and boiled down to a simple application process like President Obama's recent action. This program may be around for a long time.

The ramifications of the new Deferred Action for Childhood Arrivals (DACA) program can be understood by reviewing the temporary benefits provided by temporary protected status, or TPS. Authorized by Section 244 of the Immigration and Nationality Act (INA), TPS gives the president power to designate countries suffering from natural disasters, wars, or internal turmoil. Once designated, citizens of those countries who are in the United States—and there are always strict requirements regarding time, physical presence, and criminal background—are able to apply for TPS. Although it is not a path to permanent residence or citizenship, once a country is designated, it takes a long time before its TPS designation under Section 244 of the INA is removed.

For example, Honduras was designated for TPS in 1999 after a hurricane. Honduran citizens in the United States at the time of the designation could apply for TPS. That hurricane happened thirteen years ago, but Honduras is still designated over and over for the TPS program about every eighteen months with no end in sight.

The glaring difference between TPS and the new DACA program is that while the federal statute provides for TPS, the DACA program is the result of administrative rule making. President Obama has bypassed Congress in a way that is clearly politically calculated to maximize the benefit to him during the reelection season.

We are all sympathetic to the difficult immigration circumstances of those who come to the United States illegally as children. However, the DACA program is not a proper solution. It raises a lot of legitimate concerns about its far-reaching consequences. Obama claims that only his administration and the federal government have the authority to establish immigration policy. But by this action, he is asking states to handle the implementation of his policy via granting state IDs, scholarships, and other benefits to persons who are still technically illegal aliens. The actual intent of this action seems to be to create political upheaval in those states who want him to enforce immigration laws.

Immigration law is complicated enough, and the DACA program will only confuse matters more. Both Republicans and Democrats defeated the Comprehensive Immigration Reform Act of 2007, but Obama could have reintroduced it in Congress while the Democrats held a supermajority between 2008 and 2010.

Obama has provided temporary work permits to illegal aliens who will compete for jobs with citizens who can't find them. Furthermore, with state-issued IDs, will these Dreamers now be able to register to vote? The DACA program is designed to help Obama's reelection bid and will do nothing to address the broader and more complicated immigration issues facing our country.

Amnesty Is Not the Solution

Immigration

National columnist Ruben Navarrette recently claimed in one of his editorials that Washington politicians have no clue about immigration, but apparently he doesn't either. Navarrette is one among many Hispanics who are taking an amnesty-or-nothing approach to immigration policy in light of the recent elections. However, their approach is shortsighted and isn't right for American workers and taxpayers.

Our national immigration laws are in dire need of revision and change. They are a patchwork of policies developed when our nation was young, expanding, and more agricultural than it is today. There were employment opportunities for unskilled workers and people with limited education.

However, today, education and technical training are very much in demand. A worker must at least have the ability to read and write instructions and follow directions. America also has a great need for employees who have higher-level math skills.

What we don't need are more poorly educated, unskilled workers. We don't need immigrants who take more out of the system than they contribute. Our nation cannot afford to admit anyone and everyone. And here is the new shocking reality: we must be selective in our immigration policy. Amnesty (the new code phrase is "pathway to citizenship") is the wrong solution.

We had amnesty in 1986 for more than three million persons who had entered the United States illegally. It was supposed to be coupled with enforcement, which apparently didn't work because now we are talking about ten to fifteen million illegal aliens partaking of a new amnesty program.

Before the politicians start talking about a new amnesty program or pathway to citizenship, they must first look to enforcement. That was part of the 1986 Immigration Reform Act that was never fully instituted.

Along with enforcement, we should create a new guest worker program for immigrants who want to work. This program can help bring the many illegal aliens currently employed in the underground economy out of the shadows. This would allow federal officials to learn who is here and register these persons. But it should not be a pathway to citizenship.

Second, we must rewrite the out-of-date immigration laws and policies to fit the needs of the US economy in the twenty-first century. Instead of trying to reunify families, as in the nineteenth century, we need to encourage the immigration of highly educated and skilled people.

We don't need more unskilled immigrants who will cost taxpayers billions of dollars and deprive Americans of jobs. Why would we legalize millions of illegal immigrants when we have record deficits and chronic unemployment?

Congress should take steps to improve our immigration system. We could open up jobs for unemployed American workers by requiring all businesses to use E-Verify, an electronic program identifying illegal immigrants in the workforce and protecting jobs for legal workers. That's a commonsense solution, and the public widely supports it.

While Navarrette consults with illegal immigrant advocates, it seems he could learn a lot from the common American workers and citizens, too.

When Is Amnesty Not Amnesty?

Immigration

When is a pathway to citizenship not amnesty or a reward? Over the past few weeks, some conservatives and Republicans have criticized me for confusing the two terms. I have expressed my concern that some Texas Tea Party groups, like the San Antonio Tea Party, may have bought off on the idea that there is a difference between a pathway and amnesty.

However, in my opinion, anyone who willfully entered the country illegally should not be eligible for citizenship ever. My reasons for this hard position are as follows:

1. Unless there is a severe and costly penalty to willful illegal entry, the problem will continue forever. This second adjustment for the millions of illegal immigrants will only lead to a third, fourth, and so forth because there is no absolute penalty for illegal entry.
2. Conservatives seem to be falling into the trap where liberals keep moving the goalpost in this game. Instead of staking a position and holding strong, conservatives and Republicans are moving left and accepting a pathway that will lead to higher taxes for social services.
3. Conservatives and Republicans do not understand the impact Univision and Telemundo are having on Spanish-speaking immigrants. Both TV networks routinely make MSNBC and

7

other liberal media look conservative in the manner they report on immigration issues. Their reporters pander to their Spanish-speaking audience and portray them as victims. Furthermore, they always refer to conservatives as "anti-imigrante" as if everyone who wants to secure the border is anti-immigration. This constant biased reporting is raising a generation of Hispanics who will distrust anyone or anything conservative or Republican and will vote accordingly. If conservatives and Republicans think future generations of Hispanics will vote for them if they provide a pathway, they are very mistaken.

4. A fear of the Hispanic vote seems to be driving conservatives and Republicans to compromise, and they seem to be falling headlong into compromise with the left. Fear should never be the motivation behind public policy or political action.

A friend in the San Antonio Tea Party leadership recently told me that my position on disqualifying anyone who entered the United States illegally after 1987 was unreasonable. He feels a pathway is necessary. I have also been told that my suggestion that foreign countries should pay us for their citizens who are here illegally by forfeiting their foreign aid is unreasonable. I guess I'm an unreasonable person when it comes to the law and taxes.

However, I feel conservatives, particularly Tea Party types, should stand by their principles and not react to liberals' efforts to control the argument. Many conservative Mexican Americans oppose amnesty in any form, and they should be heard. Yes, I believe we can have a guest worker program, and yes, we need to fix the entire immigration process, but we should not reward illegal entry into the United States with any form of amnesty or citizenship.

Message for LULAC: Mexican Immigrants Need Assimilation, Not Separation

Immigration

The current immigration debate reminds me of some lessons lost in history. My father organized a printers' union in Laredo, Texas, in the 1940s to keep Mexican illegal aliens from taking Americans' jobs. Amazingly, seventy years later, liberals are claiming Mexican Americans and illegal aliens have mutual social, political, and economic goals. I disagree with them totally.

For example, when my father was young, the League of United Latin American Citizens (LULAC) pursued a very different goal than it does today. Author Benjamin Marquez verifies this in his book, *Constructing Identities in Mexican-American Political Organizations: Choosing Issues, Taking Sides*. LULAC's original goal in 1929 was to promote the full assimilation of its members into US Anglo-Saxon culture. They believed assimilation, the same pathway as every other immigrant group, was the best strategy to combat discrimination in south Texas. They even asserted that it was not the economic or political intuitions that were flawed, but discrimination was the result of racism alone.

LULAC promoted capitalism and individualism and believed that Mexican Americans could improve themselves through hard work and assimilation. They emphasized American patriotism and asserted that Mexican Americans should disavow any allegiance to Mexico, remain permanently in the United States, and commit fully to the democratic ideals of the United States. Their patriotism was evident by the group's official song, "America." They claimed its official language as English and even used its official prayer as the "George Washington Prayer."

However, since the 1970s, liberals claim the system is the problem and Mexican Americans and Mexican aliens are victims of the same class struggle against capitalism and racism. Groups like National Council of La Raza and the AFL-CIO have partnered to promote cultural separatism. Saul Alinsky groups like Valley InterFaith and COPS/Metro have organized local groups to further their economic and political agenda.

Still other groups like Mexican American Legal Defense and Education Fund (MALDEF) have fought legal battles for voting rights and representation that only segregate Mexican Americans instead of integrating and assimilating them. New leaders such as the mayor of San Antonio, Julian Castro, and his twin, US Congressman Joaquin Castro, like to speak about Hispanic and Latino issues, as if Cuban Americans, Puerto Ricans, and Central and South Americans all have the same history, national identity, and socioeconomic status.

Texans of Mexican descent have been displaced socially, economically, and politically by Mexican aliens since the US-Mexican border was created. Mexican Americans moved north to places like Chicago and Kansas City because Mexican aliens depressed the standard of living in south Texas. Poor and undereducated Mexican Americans have suffered the most from this competition, but liberals want to lump them together for their own political gain.

Billions of public dollars have been spent on south Texas since the War on Poverty began in the 1960s, and it is still poor because of the uncontrolled Mexican influx into the region. To help poor Mexican Americans in south Texas, we need a secure border and an assimilation policy for all immigrants. I am proud of my Mexican (not Hispanic or Latino) heritage, but I am Texan and American first, thanks to my parents.

Mexico Is Not Behaving like a Friend

Border Security

Mexico is not behaving like a good neighbor or a friend because one of their citizens, who was here illegally, faced justice in Texas. In December 2013, Secretary of State John Kerry intervened to delay the execution of a convicted Mexican national in Texas, saying his rights might have been violated in a case that could endanger Americans abroad, a US official said.

Edgar Arias Tamayo, who was found guilty of the 1994 fatal shooting of a Houston police officer, was set to be put death by the state of Texas. But Kerry had warned that he was not given his right to see Mexican consular officials, as the United States is obligated to do under an international convention.

Someone should explain to Kerry that our problem is not Mexican nationals on death row, but better border security and a Mexican government that is not a good neighbor. Kerry should be preaching to Mexico, not Texas, about international obligations because our neighbor to the south is not behaving in a neighborly manner on many fronts.

For example, in a forty-eight-hour period in late 2013, the following crimes were reported on the Texas-Mexico border:

- On Monday, December 16, sixty-one pounds of cocaine were seized in Pharr from a car carrying a Mexican family into Texas.
- In Laredo, also on Monday, a former Mexican police officer was charged with possession of marijuana.
- In Hildago, on Tuesday, December 17, $350,000 in cash was seized as another Mexican national tried to smuggle bundles of money into Mexico.
- Also, on Tuesday, US law enforcement seized $323,000 in heroin being smuggled into the United States by a Mexican man.
- In Laredo, on Tuesday, an eighteen-year-old illegal alien who had been deported numerous times, led Laredo police on a car chase through the city before being caught.
- In El Paso, federal agents completed a two-month operation that confiscated nearly $3.5 million in counterfeit merchandise that had come from China through Mexico into the United States.
- There was the recent report of the former governor of the Mexican state of Coahuila who had been arrested in the United States for money laundering and smuggling.

These incidents do not include the ongoing problems Texas and the United States have had lately with Mexico not honoring its formal treaties on water use regarding the Rio Grande. Even a Mexican fishing boat was recently chased from American waters along the south Texas coast.

All this, and Kerry was worried about our relationship with Mexico over a convicted cop killer in Texas? Here's a news flash: Mexico has not behaved like a good neighbor in some time. And Kerry, President Obama, and all the other globalist liberals should worry about securing and protecting our borders.

If Mexico were a good neighbor, they would respect our laws and help stop the crime. Instead criminal activity and illegal entry flourish while the Mexican government looks the other way.

The *Texas Tribune* has reported that immigration and border crime are the top concerns for Texans in 2013. As the 2014 elections near, all Texans should recognize which politicians are pandering for votes and which want to honestly address the problems because Mexico is not behaving like a friend or a good neighbor.

The Border Crisis Worsens

Immigration and Border Security

The news from the *Texas Rio Grande Valley* today is noteworthy for how the event is being described. The politically correct mainstream media and politicians who do not want to offend Latinos are avoiding the word *invasion*. They also don't want to upset the American public with an accurate description.

Instead the politicians and the media are emphasizing the word *humanitarian*. It is designed to show compassion for the victims of a failed US immigration policy, which needs to be fixed—that is, "reformed." Ultimately America is again blamed for a problem originating in another country, and of course we will need to spend money to fix it.

By calling it a humanitarian crisis, the media and politicians are also setting up the public for some sort of broad immigration action. Whether it is called amnesty or a temporary stay, it will have the same impact on the taxpayer. If a temporary status for adults is granted and if a new version of the DACA program is created for minors, hundreds of thousands of illegal immigrants will be able to stay in the United States indefinitely while the government (the taxpayer) provides benefits. And because it is defined as humanitarian crisis, there will be less public opposition.

Texas's state government is attempting to address the problem, but this appears to be more political theater than substantive action. Texas law enforcement will be stopping the criminals, but not detaining—never mind deporting—illegal aliens.

However, illegal aliens continue to be the responsibility of the federal Border Patrol, and because Obama has neutered immigration law enforcement, any illegal aliens who are apprehended are being released. For example, if a criminal (drug or human smuggler) is caught with ten illegal aliens, he is arrested, but the illegals are released. This does not equal border security or immigration law enforcement.

So what should our government do, if it were to act?

1. Immediately deport all illegal aliens, including mothers with children, and unaccompanied minors.
2. Enforce the employer sanctions law that punishes employers for hiring illegal aliens.
3. Suspend all trade, treaties, and foreign aid to nations whose citizens are coming as illegal aliens, and keep that money to protect its own borders.
4. Demand that Mexico stop the illegal immigration through its country and/or suspend all trade, treaties, and foreign aid until it does.
5. Stop providing benefits for all illegal aliens in the United States, including Dreamers.
6. Build a fence and use the military to protect our national borders.
7. Demand that Univision, Telemundo, and other US-based Spanish-language media report this crisis fairly and accurately to discourage more illegal immigration from Latin America.
8. Vote out all the Democrats in November, and then weed out the RINOs!

My family has lived with illegal immigration and border crime for six generations in south Texas. We have seen how Democratic Party bosses manipulate the poor and uneducated illegal aliens for their political gain.

I also worked on the 1986 Immigration Act, and I saw firsthand how the US Chamber and many Republican business elites fought against the enforcement of immigration laws because they wanted cheap labor and easy border crossings for trade.

Substantive action must be taken. In the meantime, we the people should prepare to act on our own to protect and preserve our state and nation.

Is It an Invasion or a Humanitarian Crisis?

Immigration

It is interesting how the mainstream media and politicians are describing events in the Texas Rio Grande Valley. They call it a *humanitarian crisis* while avoiding the word *invasion*.

By calling it a humanitarian crisis, politicians and the media emphasize the compassion for the illegal aliens who become victims of a failed US immigration policy that needs to be fixed, or "reformed." On the other hand, by avoiding the use of the word *invasion*, the mainstream media doesn't upset the American public with an accurate description of the event, and the politicians don't offend potential Latino voters. But regardless of what it is called, hundreds of thousands of illegal aliens have entered our country since January, and many more continue to enter daily.

The fact is that the federal government has failed to control our national borders. Stopping and deporting illegal aliens continues to be the responsibility of the Border Patrol, but because President Obama has played politics with immigration law enforcement, any illegal aliens who are apprehended are being released.

In Texas, the state government is attempting to address the illegal entry of so many aliens, but this appears to be more political theater than substantive action. Texas law enforcement will be stopping the criminals, but not detaining (never mind deporting) illegal aliens.

For example, if a criminal (drug or human smuggler) is caught with ten illegal aliens, he is arrested, but the illegals are released. This does not equal border security or immigration law enforcement. But then again, it's not an invasion.

Because it is a humanitarian crisis, federal money will be spent in bundles. The mainstream media and the politicians will scramble to be good humanitarians. We can be sure there will be some sort of executive action by Obama on behalf of these illegal aliens, and of course, the American taxpayer will pay for it.

The majority of these adult illegal aliens are poor and uneducated, and many are single women with children. They will need long-term social services and public assistance for housing, food, and medicine. The unaccompanied minors will have the same needs as the adults, plus education and adult supervision. We can anticipate the politicians creating a new and expanded version of the DREAM Act for them.

Barak Obama promised to fundamentally change America. The rule of law does not exist for him. In a game of football, you must go ten yards to get a first down while he has just gone five yards. For the past six years, his administration has picked and chosen which laws to uphold and which to ignore on every front, including immigration.

By calling this crisis a humanitarian crisis, liberals in the media hope to create a sense of guilt in the American public to lessen the opposition to their spending of more taxpayer money. That may work. Hopefully people will realize that what we truly need is to protect America's borders and enforce immigration laws, which means stopping the invasion and deporting the illegal aliens.

Comparing Apples and Bowling Balls

Civil Rights and Immigration

Once again, President Obama is bending history to fit his agenda. One moment he and his open-borders supporters are calling illegal aliens "the new civil rights movement," similar to African Americans in the 1960s. The next moment they claim Latino illegal aliens in America are like Joseph, Mary, and Jesus seeking refuge in Egypt. On St. Patrick's Day, Obama compared Latino illegal aliens to the Irish immigration experience, another attempt to rewrite history to fit his liberal agenda.

The truth is that there are some very big and important differences in the two immigrations.

1. The Irish had to cross an ocean to get to America, and their entry was controlled. Latinos are just next door with no large, visible geographical barrier, and their entry has never been as controlled.

2. The Irish came in numbers small enough to assimilate and become Americanized. On the other hand, for every one Latino that assimilates and Americanizes, five, six, or more have just crossed the border. And assimilation and Americanization does not seem to be their goal in recent times. Additionally, the Latino immigration numbers are overwhelming in comparison to the Irish or any other immigrant group.

3. The Irish never had Celtic language media that helped them keep and maintain their national and ethnic identity separate

from the rest of America. Latinos have Spanish-language media, which helps to segregate them and, in some cases, even discourages their assimilation. Spanish-language media, along with the liberal mainstream media, often portray Latino immigrants as "victims in and of America," which lessens their desire to become part of the new nation. There is also the narrative, particularly among liberal academics, that Texas and the southwestern United States is "occupied Mexico."

4. There is the obvious difference in that the Irish did not have political correctness to hinder their integration and assimilation to become Americans. Latino illegal aliens are neither integrating nor assimilating. Rather they are encouraged to segregate, separate, and maintain their national identity.

5. There is the fact that Latino or Hispanic are manufactured identities. While African Americans and Irish are real racial and nationality groups, there is no such thing as Latino or Hispanic. Latinos/Hispanics are an amalgamation of various racial and national Spanish-speaking groups. Their main commonality is language. Even Filipinos have been classified as Latino/Hispanic.

Comparing today's Latino immigration experience to the Irish immigration experience is like comparing apples and bowling balls. Both have a similar shape, but they're radically different in functionality.

Local Law Enforcement, Illegal Immigration, and Sanctuary Cities

Immigration

The role of local law enforcement in supporting federal immigration laws (or not) is an issue of intense discussion in this political season. It is a fact of life that people who hide usually have done something wrong. Illegal aliens hide from law enforcement because they have done something wrong. That is, they entered the country illegally, without permission, "sin papels."

If someone has broken the law, however minor it may seem to some people, he has indeed broken the law and should face the consequences. If a person has entered the country illegally, he has broken the law. That is simple and logical.

Supporters of sanctuary cities justified the ignoring of one crime to solve another. Local law enforcement often claim that illegal aliens help solve crimes and therefore are not turned over to federal immigration officials. They often claim immigration laws are not in their jurisdiction and therefore turn a blind eye to illegal aliens even when they identify them.

However, if a law enforcement agency that does not have enforcement jurisdiction over a given law finds a violation, that agency should alert or inform the appropriate agency that has jurisdiction because all law enforcement agents should be interested in enforcing all laws.

Claiming that illegal aliens help to solve crimes is like saying criminals should be given a pass because they help solve other crimes. Criminals are criminals, and lawbreakers are lawbreakers, whether the offense is major or not.

Furthermore, the sheer number of illegal aliens in the United States today is overwhelming enough without providing safe havens in communities where local law enforcement does not cooperate or support federal immigration laws. Local law enforcement should not pick and choose which laws they will enforce or support.

Illegal aliens are hiding because they did something wrong, and all law enforcement agents, whether local, state, or federal, should be interested in any law that has been broken. Law enforcement agents should not be political in determining which law they will enforce or with which law enforcement agencies they will cooperate.

During prohibition, many communities had law enforcement agents that ignored bootleggers. They were either in league with the criminals or simply chose to look the other way. In either case, it contributed directly or indirectly to the lawlessness.

If a segment of society does not like a given law, they should change it through the proper and legal process rather than encourage lawlessness. It is very important that all law enforcement agents be above politics. Law and order depends on the enforcement of all laws, and our society depends on it to ensure the domestic tranquility.

What part of the word *illegal* don't they understand?

Hispanic Conservatives Warn the GOP about Immigration and Trump

Immigration and Politics

A group of Hispanic Republicans that the mainstream media calls "conservative" have portrayed Americans of Latino descent as a single-issue, monolithic group of voters who are primarily concerned about immigration. I call these Hispanic Republicans "professional Hispanics" because they make a living off being Hispanic and claiming to be experts on all things Hispanic.

These Hispanic leaders held a press conference before GOP presidential debate to proclaim there is a "Republican-Latino problem." They seem to care more about their ethnicity than about the Constitution, the rule of law, or the meaning of the word *illegal*. Not surprisingly most of these folks are Jeb Bush supporters and criticize Donald Trump and Ted Cruz.

Among this group of Hispanic leaders was the LIBRE Initiative, a faith-based group funded by the libertarian Koch brothers who oppose immigration restrictions in the name of free and cheap labor. Sadly they use religion to justify illegal immigration.

Their main worry is the strong comments on immigration and the border security, particularly from Trump. Under the pretext of representing the Hispanic community, they made broad statements to the mainstream media about the danger of the GOP "losing inroads into the Hispanic community." However, these Hispanic leaders ignored several facts:

1. Hispanics/Latinos are not a monolithic voting racial / ethnic / national origin group. Puerto Ricans, Mexican Americans, Cubans, Central Americans, and other Latinos are all different. There are Mexicans who just crossed the border and Mexican Americans who have been in the United States for several generations, even centuries. Racially, there are Hispanics of European, African, and indigenous descent and every mixture in between. They also all have a different immigration experience. These differences keep them from being a unified voting block.

2. The majority of Americans, including Americans of Latino descent, are concerned about illegal immigration. What's the point of being a citizen if the same rights, privileges, and benefits of citizenship go to people who broke the law to enter the country?

3. Illegal immigration is not a Hispanic issue. It is an American issue. It endangers the national and personal security of all Americans, including those of Hispanic/Latino descent. We must control alien entry and prevent the entry of all foreigners, especially terrorists and criminals.

4. Illegal aliens compete for jobs with lower-skilled American workers, including poor blacks and Hispanics. Before a guest worker program is discussed, we should have welfare reform and enforcement of laws that prevent the hiring of illegal aliens. Americans should always be given preference to work.

5. We cannot and must not reward illegal immigration in any form or fashion. Creating a pathway to citizenship for illegal aliens is rewarding it, and it will only encourage more illegal immigration.

6. We must secure the border and stop the magnets that bring and keep illegal aliens in our country, such as welfare,

employment, and education. We should also deport all illegal aliens regardless of age as soon as they are apprehended.

7. We are turning our nation into the world's orphanage by allowing illegal unaccompanied minors to stay in the country and then to reward those who send them here with family reunification.

8. Many more Americans of Hispanic descent identify with the United States and want their nation protected and its borders controlled, and they want to stop rewarding illegal aliens.

These Hispanic GOP conservatives who warned the GOP and who criticized Ted Cruz and Donald Trump are little more than political dinosaurs who used their ethnicity to gain special favor and attention. It's also not surprising that liberal mainstream media ran with their story widely.

The Republican Party should start respecting and responding to the will of the people, which wants illegal immigration stopped. Even Americans of Hispanic descent want it stopped because it's not a Hispanic issue, but an American one. After all, what part of the word *illegal* don't they understand?

Reasons against Sanctuary Cities

Illegal Immigration and Law Enforcement

Leftists and the liberal media, especially the Spanish-language media, have used emotional arguments to support sanctuary cities and to "protect innocent illegal aliens." However, reason, logic, and the law provide the reasons why sanctuary cities are illegal and should be opposed:

1. Illegal immigration is not a race or ethnic issue. It is a national security issue. Anyone who cries racism is doing so out of desperation and a lack of facts. It is an emotional argument, not a logical defense, because a sovereign nation has the right to determine who enters its borders.

2. Sanctuary cities facilitate and encourage illegal immigration. They are magnets that encourage and justify illegal behavior, and they are unfair to legal immigrants who followed the rules and showed respect for the law.

3. What's the point of being a citizen or a legal resident if the illegal aliens get the same rights, privileges, and benefits?

4. Sanctuary cities impose costs on citizens and legal immigrants in the form of tax dollars that ought properly to benefit them. On the other hand, they go to underwrite hospital, police, prison, and education services for illegal aliens.

5. These communities promote crime and jeopardize citizens and legal residents. A 2005 study by the US Government Accountability Office (GAO) examined the cases of more than

fifty-five thousand illegal immigrants incarcerated in federal, state, and local facilities. The study found that these illegal alien criminals had been previously arrested an average of eight times each. Almost all of them had been convicted of a felony, with a fifth for drug offenses, and many for violent crimes. The first and primary role of the federal, state, and local governments is to protect its citizens.

6. They burden and endanger the police. Contrary to what liberals and the media say, illegal aliens are not necessary to do good police work. Police in sanctuary cities have a revolving door of people who are arrested for various criminal acts and who are in this country illegally.

7. Sanctuary cities breed disrespect for immigration laws and create an attitude of resistance for law and order. Neither law enforcement nor elected officials should ever determine which laws to enforce or not. If politicians want to create sanctuaries against immigration laws, why not create them against *Roe v. Wade* or paying taxes?

Ensuring domestic tranquility, as per the Constitution, presupposes that all persons will obey all laws, including those who disagree with it. If they disagree with a law, a legal and proper process can be followed to change it.

However, they are not free to thumb their nose at the law, much less tell police officers that they must follow illegal and irresponsible policies that are based on politics and endanger citizens. We cannot excuse and/or reward illegal immigration in any way, or we will get more. What part of word *illegal* don't they understand?

Citizens need to address sanctuary cities at the local level because they are the result of actions by local elected officials against federal immigration policies. Sanctuary cities must be opposed because they are lawless and encourage lawlessness. Elected officials who swear to support the Constitution should do that.

I Witnessed Immigration Laws Undermined

Illegal Immigration

I had the great privilege of working for President Reagan in various capacities in his administration. In 1985–87, I worked for Commissioner Alan Nelson at the former Immigration and Naturalization Service (INS) in the Department of Justice as a special assistant. My job was to help develop and implement the 1986 Immigration Reform Act that included employer sanctions for hiring illegals; prohibited federal funds for grants, programs, or services that served illegals; provided for speedy deportation of all illegals apprehended regardless of age, particularly criminals; and included a one-time amnesty program. Except for the last part, it was a pretty good law.

In 1989, I went to work for Jack Kemp at the US Department of Housing and Urban Development (HUD) in the George H. W. Bush administration. Three months into the administration, Kemp received a call from Senator Pete Wilson (R-California) about the city of Costa Mesa. Costa Mesa was upset it could not use HUD Community Development Block Grant (CDBG) and public housing funds because many of their recipients were illegals. Professional GOP Hispanics, who live off being Hispanic experts, immediately jumped on the issue, claiming the Hispanic vote for Republicans would suffer if the law weren't waived.

Slowly over the next few months, I watched as the Bush White House had every single federal program, including education, agriculture, labor, and health and human services, waive the portion of the law that prevented federal funds from serving illegal aliens. By 2008, even speedy deportation was gone, and America had magnets that brought and kept illegals in the United States.

Today, on Wednesday, January 25, President Trump told Immigration and Customs Enforcement (the new INS) employees that new laws are not necessary. We should simply enforce the ones we have. I hope they return to the original 1986 Immigration Reform Act and start there. Where once we had a trickle of illegal aliens, we now have a flood, and we will need more enforcement and security, like a wall and well-equipped patrol agents.

Interestingly Wilson served as senator until 1991, and California has never had another Republican at a statewide office since. Waiving the immigration laws didn't help Republicans with the Hispanic vote, I guess.

January 27, 2017

Mexico's Tantrum

Immigration and Border Security

The Democrats, big business interests, some Republicans, and of course the anti-Trump, liberal media are freaking out over President Trump's proposed 20 percent import tax for goods from Mexico. They feel Trump has insulted a close ally and friend. However, it's time that the United States sent a strong message regarding illegal immigration and border security to Mexico to get their attention. If an import tax and a wall can do it, so be it. Let's understand some facts:

1. Mexico has not respected the US-Mexico border since it was created in 1848. Mexican illegal immigration and contraband have become a cultural norm along the border, and Mexican ballads (*corridos*) even celebrate illegal aliens and criminals like medieval sagas.

2. Mexico suffers from a national US inferiority complex. An old Mexican saying says, "Poor Mexico. So far from God and so close to the United States," which summarizes their problems. Mexican leaders are quick to blame the United States for all their political and economic ills instead of honestly correcting the corruption that has become an acceptable part of their political culture.

3. Because of this Gringo complex, Mexico has been slow to honor any treaties or agreements with federal government or any of the states. They have not honored basic water and air pollution treaties with Texas, and their fishing boats regularly violate American waters.

4. American big business interests like the local, state, and national Chambers of Commerce are upset with a possible trade war. Big business has profited greatly from unfair trade situations with Mexico and other nations.

Globalism hurts Texas and American workers, along with small businesses and local economies. Americans workers and small businesses cannot compete with cheap Mexican labor and economy.

Finally, we must ask: what does Mexico produce that Texas or America cannot? If burdensome government regulations are removed, there is nothing Texas and the rest of the United States cannot produce. Texans and all Americans should have the economic freedom and power to produce and consume as best they can without government interference and globalist policies.

Mexico is acting like a spoiled child that is told no for the first time and responds by throwing a tantrum. The Mexican government has done little to stop illegal immigration, and it has done nothing to create a fair trade relationship with the United States.

It's time that we send a strong message to Mexico to get their attention. Texas and America first!

Mexican Presidential Candidate Holds Anti-Trump Rally in LA

Immigration and Border Security

Imagine if a stranger came to your home and criticized you to your family. That's what happened in Los Angeles last Sunday, February 12, when Mexican presidential candidate, Andres Manuel López Obrador, held a rally and criticized President Trump's plans to build a wall across the US-Mexico border.

López Obrador, who represents the ruling Institutional Revolutionary Party (PRI), said, "I think the wall and the demagoguery of patriotism are no match for the dignity and humanity of the American people." He went on to praise California as "a refuge and blessing for immigrants" and exclaimed "long live California" to the cheers of the crowd.

Many recognize that most Mexican politicians suffer a deep inferiority complex toward Texas and America. Texas defeated Santa Ana and won their independence. And the United States beat them and won half of their territory, all in an attempt to win Texas back.

The current border and immigration problems the United States has are a reflection that Mexico has never truly accepted or respected the international border. Legal and illegal commerce and immigration have flowed back and forth with little to no restraints since 1848.

After the Mexican revolution of 1910, Mexican nationalism went into high gear. In the 1920s and 1930s, politicians and artists coupled the hypernationalism with socialism and anti-capitalist, anti-Christian, and anti-American rhetoric. In 1926, President Plutarco Calles initiated a fierce backlash against Catholics, which led to the Cristero War. In 1938, President Lazaro Cardenas nationalized the Mexican oil industry, which American, British, and Dutch companies owned and managed.

López Obrador represents PRI, a Mexican political party that was founded in 1929 and held power uninterruptedly in the country for seventy-one years until 2000. The PRI participates in the Socialist International, but they are not considered a true social democratic party because they have done more to loot the people and nation of their wealth than to redistribute the wealth. In 1990, Peruvian Nobel Prize laureate for literature, Mario Vargas Llosa, called the Mexican government under the PRI *la dictadura perfecta* ("the perfect dictatorship").

While superficially Mexican politicians show a friendly face toward the United States, they are actually very insecure and envious of their neighbor to the north. Mexican politicians routinely criticize American policies toward their nation, but heaven forbid if an American politician, particularly a president like Trump, ever criticizes Mexico.

The idea of a Mexican presidential candidate criticizing an American president on American soil is repugnant. Furthermore, the American national media and the United Nations ignored this national affront. We can also assume that a California leftist arranged the visit to embarrass or provoke Trump. You can bet López Obrador would not have had the same reception in Texas.

Typical of all insecure and dishonest governments, Mexican politicians see themselves and their country's failures as faultless victims of Yankee imperialism. But it is ominous when foreigners are being bold enough to come to the United States to verbally attack us, dangerous when fellow citizens are foolish enough to host them, and destructive when the mainstream media ignores or downplays the incident.

The Trump Effect: Illegal Immigration Numbers Drop in January 2017

Immigration

Some are calling Wall Street's optimism the "Trump effect," but illegal immigration seems to be feeling the effect too. In January 2017, the first month of the Trump administration, illegal immigration crossings at the Mexican border have fallen compared to other months.

According to the figures released by Customs and Border Protection (CPB) on Monday, March 6, the number of both illegal immigrant families and children traveling alone has slowed. While the numbers are still high compared to past years, it's the lowest for January since 2012.

The total apprehensions of illegal aliens trying to cross the border fell 27 percent on a month-to-month basis, to 31,575, while the number of inadmissible aliens who presented themselves at US-Mexico ports of entry fell 28 percent to 10,899. Border Patrol officials say apprehensions are the best indicator of the overall flow: the more people caught, the more are believed to be getting through. And that's the number that fell by 27 percent.

However, these figures can be misleading because illegal entries decrease in the winter and rise up again in the spring. Last year, the Border Patrol reported that apprehensions dropped 36 percent from December 2015 to January 2016.

The drop in illegal immigration may be good news, but the CPB report said that overall total migration remained at elevated levels, primarily due to the continuing large numbers of family units and unaccompanied children from Central America, Haiti, and Cuba. In short, the illegal immigration crisis continues.

For eight years, the Obama administration directly or indirectly encouraged illegal immigration, especially from Mexico and Latin America. They excused and rewarded illegal aliens with benefits and protections while doing little to stop or discourage the flow.

Trump's "America First" policies, such as his goal of securing the Mexican border, have been met with applause and anger. Americans who have experienced the negative effects of uncontrolled immigration want the border controlled.

But leftist Americans and Mexico's leaders call border control efforts "racist." The liberal mainstream media almost daily reports about illegal aliens who live in fear of being deported. Univision's Jorge Ramos has told CNN that the Trump effect is causing a "fear stronger than any wall" that is keeping illegal immigrants from coming into the United States. Democrats lament that America's welcome mat has been replaced with a "keep out" sign.

The fear of deportation the leftists and the media clamor about is not the fault of the citizens. People who broke the law by entering the country illegally or, worse, sent an unaccompanied child into the country illegally are responsible for that crime. Yes, illegal immigration is a crime, and people who commit crimes feel fearful of being caught.

The United States, as all nations, has the right to determine who does or doesn't enter their borders. It also has a responsibility to protect its citizens first and foremost. It is shameful that leftists and the media try to scare lawful immigrants for the sake of their political agenda by lumping them in with illegal aliens.

Addressing the Dreamers Issue

Immigration

There continues to be an emotional discussion regarding Dreamers, or the foreign-born minors who have been brought into our country illegally. Dreamers are illegal aliens and should be treated as such.

The common argument on their behalf is "It is not their fault. We must not punish them." However, it's not the fault of the American citizens and taxpayers either. The fault lies with the adults who brought them and the countries that didn't care for them. There must be a consequence, or the problem will continue.

We cannot excuse and reward the illegal immigration of minors because of emotional sentiments. We cannot turn our country into the world's orphanage and let the nations of the world drop their children at our doorstep without our permission, expecting the American taxpayer to raise them. The following steps must be taken:

1. We get the attention of those countries where these minors come from and stop sending them foreign aid. That would get the attention of their national leaders. If we are going to be humanitarians, let's be humanitarians here with those minors.
2. We stop reunifying undocumented minors with undocumented adults and allowing them to stay in the United States indefinitely. That is rewarding their illegal entry into the United States.

3. We must immediately detain and deport minors stopped at the border or picked up by ICE. They should be treated the same as all undocumented aliens who are picked up.

All federal programs that provide assistance to illegal alien minors (and to all illegal aliens in general) must be stopped. These magnets bring and keep illegal aliens in the United States.

It is sad that these young people are dumped at our doorstep and that their own nations and even families expect the American taxpayer to raise them. But we cannot turn our nation into the world's orphanage. We must secure the borders and all points of entry. We must end the magnets that bring and keep illegal immigrants, including programs for minors. And we must deport all illegal aliens, including minors, and end the foreign aid with their countries of origin that do not cooperate with US immigration law and policy.

Only when these actions are taken will the United States be able to truly address the illegal immigration problem.

Obama/Holder Cover-Up of Fast and Furious and the Death of Brian Terry

Border Security

New evidence in the Fast and Furious Senate investigation has found a cover-up in the Obama administration in the death of a Border Patrol agent, Brian Terry, in December 2010. It was found that just hours after the death of Agent Terry, former attorney general Eric Holder's Justice Department tried to cover up evidence that the gun that killed Terry was one the government intentionally helped sell to the Mexican cartels in a weapons trafficking program known as Operation Fast and Furious.

This new revelation comes just days after a huge shake-up of government officials who oversaw the failed anti-gun-trafficking program and renewed demands by Congress for more answers. Senator Charles Grassley's office (R-Iowa) found that thirty-one more Fast and Furious guns were found at twelve violent crime scenes in Mexico.

In an internal email the day after Agent Terry's murder, Department of Justice assistant US attorney Emory Hurley and then US attorney Dennis Burke decided not to disclose the connection, saying, "This way we do not divulge our current case (Fast and Furious) or the Border Patrol shooting case." Clearly it was a cover-up designed to deceive the public.

Given this new revelation, south Texas citizens should demand answers from the congressional Democrats who represent the border region.

"Not only did this reckless and illegal activity jeopardize the safety of Border Patrol agents and other law enforcement officers, but Texas residents all along the border were also endangered."

Democrats have politically dominated south Texas for decades, and they should be held accountable for this lawlessness that characterized the Obama administration, as well as the unsecure and lawless border.

Democrat congressmen—Filemon Vela, Henry Cuellar, Vicente Gonzalez, and even Beto O'Rourke in El Paso—should be confronted by citizens demanding answers regarding this Obama/Holder cover-up. These Hispanic Democrats must be held accountable for what the leader of their party did. Furthermore, voters and citizens should not let them cry discrimination and racism just because they are challenged politically and held accountable.

Citizens should remember how the Obama administration targeted conservatives with the IRS, spied on journalists, blamed the Benghazi massacre on a video, and ignored the illegal use of a private server by Hillary Clinton that compromised sensitive information, along with several other illegal government activities. They should particularly remember how the Democrats in Congress have chosen to ignore these illegal actions.

During President George W. Bush's administration, leftists often voiced opposition to the Iraq War by chanting, "Bush lied, and people died." That phrase is absolutely true in the case of Fast and Furious and the Obama administration.

Citizens and voters along the south Texas border must hold the Democrats accountable on their home turf for the death of a Border Patrol agent, Obama endangering the lives of all Texas and American citizens, and their dismissive arrogance toward the matter. Citizens should be outraged.

Answering Acosta's Confrontational Comments

Immigration

Regarding CNN's Jim Acosta's comments about the new proposed immigration requirements, on Tuesday, August 1, 2017, let's understand some important points from the conservative point of view:

1. Acosta was not asking a question but pushing an agenda.
2. It seems Acosta is anti–white men.
3. What's wrong with a nation determining who is going to enter its boundaries and society?
4. All cultures and societies are not the same. Some are very backward while others flourish and allow the individual to grow and develop. Why didn't the Aztecs or Incas discover Europe? Why didn't the Zulu colonize Europe? Based on those questions, America should carefully choose who is going to enter its borders. We have enough poor and unskilled people in the United States without bringing in more.
5. For Acosta to use Emma Lazarus's poem as a basis to describe or support a certain approach to immigration policy in 2017 is stupid, dumb, and a liberal political ploy. The poem was written in 1883 when America's society and economy were radically different to 2017. In 1883, poor unskilled people could come to the United States and use their hard labor and tenacity to achieve success.

But in 2017, we not only have enough unskilled and undereducated people but also encourage culture diversity, which leads to ethnic/cultural segregation and reverse racism. It has also lead to the undermining of American patriotism.

I think that Acosta, like many of the media, is a pretentious globalist. If there are any comments that should replace the Lazarus poem, it should be, "Give me individual political and economic freedom and liberty, or give me death!" That should be taught to the rest of the world rather than globalism and open-borders liberalism.

Illegal Immigration Tragedies Are Not the Fault of US Citizens

Illegal Immigration

American taxpayers/citizens are not to blame for illegal immigration and the tragedies that sometimes occur.

Eight illegal immigrants who were being smuggled into the United States were found dead inside a sweltering eighteen-wheeler trailer parked behind a Walmart store in San Antonio, early on Sunday, July 23, while another thirty people, some suffering from heat exhaustion, were found in the trailer.[1]

Almost immediately, the local pro-open-borders leftists and their news media allies began saying this is the result of inhumane immigration laws and (of course) racism. The left never misses an opportunity to use tragedy for political purposes.

However, smuggling illegal immigrants, like smuggling drugs or any illegal contraband, is the result of criminals behaving like criminals. It also involves people who have made a decision to enter the United States illegally and who are not invited or encouraged to break the laws in any way by taxpayers/citizens.

---

[1] https://www.aol.com/article/news/2017/07/23/8-people-found-dead-in-tractor-trailer-walmart-texas/23043638/.

It also shows how magnets, like welfare assistance and free education, continue to attract illegal aliens to the United States. It should also not be overlooked that San Antonio has a mayor and most of the city council that support sanctuary city policies.

While this incident is tragic, it once again shows the need for a secure border and strong immigration laws. We need to discourage illegal immigration and send a message to all the world that we will not tolerate it.

Fortunately for the illegal aliens who survived, they will receive top-of-the-line medical assistance from American health professionals. Unfortunately for the American taxpayers, they will pay for it.

All of the surviving illegal aliens should be deported as soon as possible to send a message that discourages foreigners from risking their lives by entering the United States illegally with the help of smugglers. We should not reward or excuse illegal immigration in any form or fashion.

PART 2
Race and Politics

Answering Senator Reid: Why Would a Hispanic Vote Republican?

Politics and Race

On Tuesday, August 10, 2010, Senate Majority Leader Harry Reid spoke to Hispanic Democrats at Hermandad Mexicana in Las Vegas and questioned how Hispanics could vote Republican. He blamed them for Congress's failure to pass comprehensive immigration reform. And so, let me respond to Senator Reid.

Dear Senator Harry Reid,

Not only am I a Republican, but I am also a constitutional conservative. I believe in God and public prayer, and Democrats don't. I believe the US Constitution is a divinely inspired document. I believe in the sanctity of life, while Democrats support abortions. I believe a child should be taught morals at home and not sex education at schools. I believe morality is the foundation of a civil society. I believe in free enterprise and self-determination, while Democrats want big government, which means more and higher taxes. A government that can give you everything can also take it away.

You may think that immigration is an important issue to me as a Hispanic, but it's only important to the extent of securing the border. I also am offended that noncitizens demand rights in my country when they have broken the law to enter it. This is my country, not Mexico. I am concerned about my country, and Mexico and all foreign governments, should take care of its own citizens in their native lands.

I believe I can make my decisions about life, money, and other personal issues. I believe in self-control and self-determination. I don't need the government to protect me and to take care of me.

History has shown that Democrat political bosses such as Boss Tweed in New York City, and George and Archie Parr in south Texas used the poor and uneducated to help them maintain political and economic power. Lyndon Johnson created the War on Poverty, which only led to more people being dependent on the government. It created an entire industry based on service to the poor. No thanks. I don't need to be given anything by the government (federal, state, or local) except protection from foreign invasion or attack.

Finally, it may be difficult for you and other Democrats to understand, but I am not so socially insecure that I see racism around every corner. I feel responsible for my own actions, good and bad, and for the results of those actions. When something goes wrong in my life, I don't blame *los gringos*.

It is sad that your party uses race, gender, and income to divide our nation. Instead of inspiring people to achieve, you tell people that life, liberty, and the pursuit of happiness are beyond their control and that you must help them. You seek to help them, but all you do is retard their personal growth while expanding the poverty industry.

I could go on, but suffice for me to say, I am a Republican because I love America and what it stands for. I love the principles of personal freedom, growth, and self-determination. I believe that people should be taught good principles and left to govern themselves.

Civil Rights or Civil Revenge

Civil Rights

In the latest example of a civil rights tantrum, Latino groups and other minority groups in Texas have won the battle to redraw the congressional districts. The state's population growth added four new congressional seats. Since most of the growth was due to Hispanics, liberals feel that at least three of the new districts should go to Hispanics, as if it were a quota system.

The challenge seems to be more about segregating Latinos for political purposes than about representation. The Democratic Party is a beneficiary of the challenge by Hispanic groups who claim to be nonpartisan. This is a continuation of playing race-based politics by liberals.

Several questions need to be asked. When will Latinos and other minorities be integrated into the political process if the liberals continue to segregate them? Is the idea to give all people a voice in representative politics or to create quotas assuring that Hispanics are elected? Are Hispanics the only ones who can properly represent Hispanics?

The original intent of the law was to help elect minorities, but not a given political party. Statistics show that Hispanics have been elected in great numbers across the state at all levels from both parties. So do we still need this law? Is the law's goal "to hasten the waning of racism in American politics" or "to entrench racial differences," per Justice Anthony M. Kennedy's words?

We must also ask how this law and legal action respects the will of the people. Liberal judicial activism has overturned the legal actions of a duly elected state legislature. Texas has a state legislature that includes several Hispanics and African Americans. The fact that the legislature happens to be majority Republican is an issue of political preference, not discrimination. This conservative majority legislature was elected by a conservative majority electorate, which enacted some conservative legislation, like the voter ID law and redistricting. All actions were carried out freely and legitimately. Yet liberals and judicial activists have stopped and overturned the actions of the will of the people.

Reverse discrimination is a reality, and liberals support it for their personal political gain. It does not matter that America has elected an African American president. Liberal civil rights advocates bristle at the assertion that Obama's victory signals it is time to dismantle the Voting Rights Act and other laws.

However, Ward Connerly, a leading anti–affirmative action activist, asks, "If we can't get rid of these laws now with Obama, I don't know what yardstick we're going to use." The fact is the redistricting is more a case of civil revenge by liberals who lost state elections than it is about civil rights.

Regarding the New Redistricting Maps

Voting Rights and Politics

In regards to the interim redistricting maps released yesterday, Tuesday, February 28, 2012, by the court, the fact remains that this legal challenge is less about race and violations of the Voting Rights Act and more about race being used as an excuse and the inability of Democrats to win state and local elections.

Democrats allege that the original maps drawn by the Texas state legislature discriminated against Hispanics and other minorities. However, the original maps were drawn by a Republican and conservative majority who won state elections in 2010 in fair and open elections, electing representatives who acted on their behalf. It also elected some Hispanic Republican state representatives.

If Democrats are upset about election losses, they should blame President Obama, former Speaker of the House Nancy Pelosi, and Senate Majority Leader Harry Reid for their loss. Democrats pretend, for their own political convenience, that all Hispanics in Texas are Democrats. But it seems they only want to segregate Hispanics politically into Democrat political strongholds with political bosses.

Democrats and all political parties should work for the political, economic, and social integration of Hispanics and all minorities into American society. They should not segregate them in any form or fashion. Democrats and all politicians should stop pandering to people on the basis of race because it only divides America and creates social tensions.

This lawsuit brought by liberal Hispanic Democrats is about politics of race, not civil rights. It insults the concept of a government representing all citizens and voters. The Democratic Party in Texas and the rest of the nation should stop using Hispanics and other minorities as political pawns in their desperate effort to win elections. Whatever happened to parties running on a platform of ideas rather than on race?

March 5, 2012

Responding to *Express-News* Columnist Pimentel's Editorial

Race and Politics

Express-News columnist, O. Ricardo Pimentel, shows he is an unabashed liberal with comments that are scary in his Sunday, March 4, 2012, editorial, "Power Holds on to Power." His opinions need to analyzed and answered.

Pimentel expresses frustration at the system for redistricting and calls for an "independent redistricting commission—no legislators involved." His comments raise several questions:

1. Are there any conservative Hispanic opinion writers at the *Express-News*? The lack of local conservative Hispanic opinions in the media gives the (racist) misperception that all Hispanics are liberals.
2. Pimentel attacks the system and claims it benefits only the powerful. The fact is that voters elected the legislators who designed the redistricting maps, and those voters are free Texans/Americans who acted on their own free will according to their conscience. The system is the Texan/American voter.
3. Pimentel claims the "new interim maps mark the system as wholly corrupt." Could it be that the judges determined that the lower court judges overreached because they actually did overreach?

The Voting Rights Act itself violates the US Constitution by establishing preferential treatment of one group of citizens over other citizens. It is literally government-sanctioned racism that targets selective enforcement of the law on certain states. Furthermore, the Voting Rights Act holds a state guilty until proven innocent in complete violation of the spirit of American judicial principles.

Pimentel claims, "The system's design tilts heavily to power holding on to power. And that's what makes this all so corrupt." However, the system is designed to encourage participation, and people who want change should vote and elect representatives who will design the districts as they see fit.

Also Pimentel forgets (ignores) that Democrats dominated Texas politically for over a hundred years until the 1990s, and they discriminated against Hispanics. Now because Republicans dominate, the Democrats are conveniently crying racism.

Finally, Pimentel raises the race card. He argues the maps are unfair by "essentially ignoring the minority population growth." He assumes that, because they are minority, they are Democrats. He also writes about community cohesiveness like all minority groups are a monolithic group who only wish to live segregated with other minorities. Aren't these assumptions racist, and isn't it segregation to place minorities in minority districts?

It's time to stand up and ask, "Where are the conservative Hispanic voices in San Antonio's media?" It's also time to challenge those leftist Hispanics who continue to mislead the public with their liberal point of view, pretending to speak for all Hispanics.

Rather than having a pity party for liberal Hispanic Democrats, Pimentel should encourage them to develop campaign messages that appeal to all Americans in their new district and stop playing the race game.

Culture and Poverty

Race and Politics

Republican presidential candidate Mitt Romney was criticized for his recent comment about Palestinians' culture when he said their culture hindered their economic development. Regardless of the expected negative reaction by liberals, the fact is that development and poverty can be by-products of culture.

The facts show that Palestinian culture is the problem. Unfortunately the same can be said about any lesser culture in the world and the culture of poverty in America that traps minorities.

A culture that keeps women poor and uneducated hurts Palestinian economic growth. Tribalism also dominates over individual freedom and liberty, and affects personal development. Furthermore, there are leaders who use religion to control political, economic, and social behavior and development.

On the other hand, Israel, which was founded in 1948, has developed faster than any of its Muslim nations next door because of its culture. Liberals can argue against the existence of Israel, but they cannot deny how culture has helped people to develop economically.

Likewise, many minorities in America have been trapped in their communities because of the culture of poverty and politics. The loss of the family unit, dependence on government help, a view of themselves as victims of life, and politicians who want to use the poor as their power base have contributed to creating a culture of poverty that feeds the poverty industry.

Studies show that teens with children have a greater chance of falling into and remaining in poverty. Unfortunately government assistance has only made the situation worse by making it easier for male-less households to exist.

The media and the education system are constantly telling minorities they are victims of historical discrimination and perpetrate helplessness and anger. Rarely are minorities encouraged to integrate and assimilate into society and to appreciate academics more than entertainment and sports.

On the contrary, minority trust toward law enforcement and the legal system has been undermined. Liberals are quick to excuse minority youths who dress and act gangsta, disrespect law and authority figures, and behave violently.

In economics, the community approach versus individual self-initiative has slowed or prevented economic growth for American minorities. It is sad that the socialist message of "it takes a village" has been so widely accepted by most people in the minority community. Liberals refuse to understand that, in a communal approach, an individual can progress only as fast as the slowest (or laziest) member of the community.

The failure of the War on Poverty, waged since 1965, is that it has tried to lift communities rather than individuals while it excuses and rewards poverty. American minorities and all the people of the world need to focus on personal and economic freedom and liberty with little or no government involvement and interference.

Calling Out the Racist Liberals

Racism and Presidential Politics

In yet another shocking example of liberal racism, Vice President Joe Biden said, "In the first hundred days he's (Romney) going to let the big banks once again write their own rules ... unchain Wall Street. They're going to put y'all (speaking to a crowd that included African Americans) back in chains." What makes Biden's comment more shocking and condescending was that he feigned a southern drawl.

Imagine if Republican nominee Mitt Romney or his running mate, Congressman Paul Ryan, had made that comment. Jesse Jackson and Al Sharpton would have immediately attacked them. However, liberal racism is common and unchallenged.

In May, Texas state representative Trey Martinez Fischer said Hispanics would favor US congressman Lloyd Doggett in the general election because he has a "brown heart." As with Biden's comment, no one said or challenged the comment as racist.

Liberals are racist. Why else would they use race and ethnicity to appeal for votes? If a candidate would have used race or ethnicity in his platform in the 1950s, he would have been branded a racist. In 2012, the president uses his race to court votes. Texas state legislators justify segregated congressional districts to elect candidates of a particular race or ethnicity. Isn't that racism?

Castro, the mayor of San Antonio, is being touted as the future of Texas because he is Hispanic. His twin brother, Joaquin, is favored to win a Hispanic district for a congressional seat. Playing the race card comes easily to them. Their mother, Rosie Castro, was a member of the militant Hispanic group, Raza Unida Party, in the 1970s.

In another example of liberal racism, Texas state senator Leticia Van de Putte declared that the 82nd Texas legislature was anti-Hispanic because it passed the voter ID law. Someone should ask the senator if she is pro-fraud.

Also the University of Texas is fighting a legal battle to continue using race and ethnicity as factors for considering admissions to the law school. They want to continue discriminating.

Obama and his liberal party minions have divided America as never before, and it is time to confront them at the national and local level. We must ask all candidates if they believe in equal opportunity or special rights. We must demand accountability from all our national and state elected officials so they do not show favoritism to anyone because of race, ethnicity, gender, or any other feature.

Racism is racism regardless of who practices it and how or why they justify it. The civil rights laws were passed fifty-seven years ago, and it is time to encourage unity and equality rather than division and hatred. We must tell liberals to stop the racism.

A Clear Difference in Philosophy

Race and Politics

On Wednesday evening, September 5, former president Bill Clinton spoke at the Democratic National Convention on national television. He laid out the differences in the vision of America between Democrats and Republicans and asked what kind of country people wanted to live in.

Clinton said Democrats and Obama want "a country of shared opportunities and shared responsibilities." He called it a "we're all in it together" society. That sounds wonderful and like a unified nation.

However, the reality is that Obama's actions the last three years have divided the nation by race, ethnicity, gender, sexual orientation, class, and even immigration status. The only thing Obama has accomplished in bringing the nation together is in debt.

President Clinton accused Republicans of wanting to change voting procedures "just to reduce the turnout of younger, poorer, minority and disabled voters." This was a reference to the voter ID laws that several states, including Texas, have passed to stop voter fraud. Democrats consider it evil to ask someone for proper ID when voting.

However, President Clinton and other Democrats ignore that photo IDs were required to attend most of their convention events and their delegates needed to show proper photo ID to vote. "Unions also require proper photo IDs to vote in their elections, as do many other organizations." But we can only surmise that Democrats oppose proper voter IDs because they really do support voter fraud for public elections.

Then there's the reference President Clinton made to DREAM Act. He said Obama had opened "the doors of American opportunity to young immigrants brought here as children."

The fact is that Obama has circumvented the Constitution to pander to liberal Hispanics. He and his party controlled Congress and the White House for two years, and they never acted on immigration reform. By giving a stay-of-deportation to illegal immigrants, he insulted the thousands of immigrants who followed the law while rewarding those who broke it.

President Clinton concluded by speaking of a "shared prosperity, where the middle class is growing and poverty is declining." This statement reflected the communal approach or vision Democrats and liberals have of the perfect society and what America should be. But this is also the point of greatest difference between Republicans and Democrats, between liberal and conservative. It was obvious in both conventions.

Liberals say the middle class is the ultimate goal for all Americans, and they want to use the government as the vehicle to accomplish that goal. The government is good, and therefore taxing and spending for government programs to help people is good.

Liberals prey on socially insecure people, and they ignore the fact that government doesn't create what it gives to you, but rather takes from those who create it to give it to you.

To rephrase President Clinton's speech, if you're okay with living off someone else's work, vote for Obama, Lloyd Doggett, Joaquin Castro, or any Democrat who supports this thinking.

Affirmative Action: It's Time to Pull the Plug

Race and Civil Rights

When Sonia Sotomayor was confirmed to the US Supreme Court in 2009, it was obvious to most Americans that she was not the most qualified person for the job. But it was also obvious that, because she would be the first Hispanic on the court, no one was going to seriously challenge her nomination. Thus we see the legacy of affirmative action, people who are promoted because they are members of a protected class, not because they are the best qualified.

Affirmative action may have started out as a good idea in the early 1960s to overcome discriminatory practices, but the idea soon lost its way. Its goals were redefined "to promote actions that achieve non-discrimination" and "to promote anti-discriminatory actions." Bingo! At that point, it began encouraging and justifying discrimination.

Almost fifty years and two generations of Americans later, affirmative action has expanded to include anyone and everyone who feels socially insecure because of his or her race, ethnicity, gender, national origin, religion, sexual preference, physical abilities, and even weight and height.

The fact is that affirmative action has bred discrimination. It has caused Americans to think about their differences, not commonalities. It has caused us to think tribal. Americans are encouraged to celebrate diversity, but in reality, they are taught to practice and justify a new, subtle (sometimes not so subtle) form of discrimination.

Today, Americans are identified by whether or not they are members of a protected group or class because that means having special rights and privileges. However, affirmative action, in the cold reality of day, means "discrimination."

Because affirmative action pretends to make up for past injustices, it should be called *civil revenge*, not civil rights. After fifty years of civil rights enforcement, after two generations of promoting antidiscriminatory actions, how much longer do we need this type of legal protection?

Furthermore, it has hurt protected classes by breeding the false expectations of special treatment in all their social, economic, and political activities. It is undeniable that President Obama has accomplished most of his achievements because he is African American. Many people openly admit that they voted for Obama in 2008 because of his race, not qualifications. Just look at what the ultimate affirmative action candidate has brought America because he is of a protected class, not because he is qualified.

Thus, it should be disturbing to Americans that many liberals promote politicians just because they are minorities or women. Many Democrats justify Hillary Clinton's candidacy for president because she's a woman, and others support San Antonio's mayor, Julian Castro, for vice president simply because he is Hispanic.

The case before the US Supreme Court, *Fisher v. University of Texas*, is about UT defending and justifying the preferential treatment of some at the expense of qualified people. It is time for affirmative action to end and to return to the pure principles of equal protection under the law. Competition is good, and discrimination in any form and for any reason against anyone is bad.

Ryan Guillen: Old Politics in New Bottles

Hispanics and Texas Politics

The Eagle Ford Shale oil field is creating an economic boom for south Texas, but it is also causing some political concerns.

The history of south Texas, particularly Duval County, is one of families who controlled local government with their political and economic power. The Parr family in 1900s, first Archie and then his son George, controlled politics by controlling public works contracts and access to government policymaking positions. They could get you elected, like when they elected Lyndon Johnson to the US Senate in 1948 with a stuffed ballot box, or defeat you, like when they defeated Congressman Richard Kleberg in 1945 because he crossed Parr.

However, the Parrs did not act alone. They had allies. Olivero P. (O. P.) Carrillo was a Parr ally who served as judge of the 229th District Court (Duval, Jim Hogg, and Starr Counties) before he was impeached by the Texas Senate and removed from office in 1976 for abuse of power and misuse of county funds. The charges alleged Carrillo and his brothers used a phony business to illegally sell items to Duval County and used fake invoices from the store to obtain illegal payments from county and state funds.

The Chicano movement in 1970s brought political change to south Texas. In 1957, one Mexican American was serving in the Texas legislature, but in 2001 there were forty-one. The vast majority of local elected officials in south Texas are Mexican Americans.

Old political machines ended, but new ones were created. While old political bosses were voted out, wealthy families that supported them remained, and new political bosses replaced the old ones, all of them Democrats.

The Chicano movement rattled the south Texas establishment in the 1970s, but today the conservative grassroots movement led by the Tea Party is causing political angst. A good example of this clash is the Ryan Gullien-Ann Matthews race.

Guillen considers himself a conservative Democrat, while grassroots conservatives, including the Tea Party, back Matthews. However, there is a big difference between the conservative Democrats of old and today's radical liberals.

Conservative Democrats like Lyndon Johnson praised God and embraced patriotism. They opposed America's enemies rather than apologize to them. The biggest danger to Eagle Ford Shale is Obama's energy policy, which seeks to protect bugs and reptiles instead of creating jobs, wealth, and energy independence for south Texans.

In 2009, Guillen received a 92 percent rating from the Sierra Club, and in 2011, he received a 73 percent rating. When Guillen's voting tendencies are combined with the old-style political boss politics, the energy business in south Texas could be in trouble. Guillen must support his party's environmental platform and philosophy if he wants to move up to greater positions.

Guillen flirted with joining the Republican Party in 2009, but would this make him a conservative? Will Guillen fight against eminent domain and private property rights? Will he fight the overregulation of the energy industry? Is he supported by old family bosses who want to gain more economic and political control? Voters in south Texas should ask and research these questions and beware of wolves in conservative clothing.

Do Liberals Take Hispanics Seriously?

Race Politics

When will Hispanics learn that liberals and Democrats don't take them seriously? Three years ago, Immigration Subcommittee Chairwoman Zoe Lofgren, a Democrat from California, invited comedian Stephen Colbert to testify about immigration. Lofgren disrespected Hispanics with this stunt and mocked congressional hearings.

In other examples of cynicism and disrespect, President Obama has claimed that Republicans have prevented a comprehensive immigration bill. However, when Obama wanted to pass the health care bill, he did not need Republican support. The bill passed quickly and without debate. Remember Speaker Pelosi stating, "Let's pass it so we can find out what's in it"? Obama and other liberal Democrats care about immigration when they need Hispanic support.

Then there is Senator Harry Reid of Nevada trying to pass the DREAM Act at the last minute by attaching it to the Defense Authorization bill. Again, if Reid were sincere, why didn't he attach it to the health care bill rather than wait until the last minute before Congress recesses before an election?

Liberal Democrats have a history of disrespecting and/or ignoring the Hispanic community. Liberal Democrats claim they want equal representation for all minorities in the federal government, yet the facts show blacks far outnumber Hispanics in all federal agencies, particularly in senior-level positions. It's obvious equal opportunity does not necessarily include Hispanics. And still Hispanics support liberal Democrats.

Since 1965, when the War on Poverty began, Hispanics have gotten the short end of the stick from liberal Democrats. The dropout rate, teen pregnancy, and gang problems are higher than ever among Hispanics. Hispanic supporters of liberals and Democrats say it's better to have something from Democrats than nothing from conservative Republicans.

But what the Hispanic liberals want is federal funding for their programs that keep Hispanics poor and dependent on the government. It is a simple case of giving a man a fish so he can eat today and keeping Hispanics dependent on political bosses. The War on Poverty has created an industry of poverty with poverty pimps keeping people dependent on the government.

Also through unions and federal programs like affirmative action, liberals have tried to guarantee success for Hispanics and other minorities. However, there are no guarantees for success in real life. Only hard work can bring success.

It's time for Hispanics to try something new. The answer is to become self-sufficient and economically independent. Hispanics need a conservative revolution to move them in a new direction, one that emphasizes the development of personal wealth through lower taxes, and reduced government spending, involvement, interference, and regulations.

Finally Hispanics need to stop seeing themselves as helpless. Liberals have preyed on Hispanics by telling them that they cannot succeed without government help. The facts are that Hispanics can and will succeed if the government gets out of the way.

It's time for Hispanics to stop depending on liberal Democrats because they don't take them seriously. It's time for Hispanics to start looking toward a conservative alternative.

Republican Hispanic Elected Official Risks Alienating Grassroots Conservatives

Politics

Recently Texas State Representative Jason Villalba (R-114) from Dallas told a group of Republican women in San Antonio that the anti-immigrant rhetoric in the GOP lieutenant governor's race was alienating the Hispanic vote and that Republicans should "embrace the Hispanic electorate."

In the meantime, as of last Friday, about eighty thousand undocumented immigrants had been apprehended at the border since October 2013, the start of the fiscal year, in the Border Patrol's Rio Grande Valley Sector that runs from Brownsville to Corpus Christi. This is about a 68 percent increase for the same period from last year, according to agent Daniel Tirado, spokesman for the Border Patrol's RGV Sector.

Also, on Wednesday of this week, Houston police discovered a stash house crammed full with more than one hundred illegal immigrants. The house was so full that the occupants were sitting on top of each other and were surrounded by trash bags filled with old clothing. It is thought many of the 108 men and women found inside the 1,500-square-foot home had been brought there under a human smuggling operation.

Villalba is doing a tour of Texas communities to promote his warning to the GOP, with stops that include the Rio Grande Valley, Corpus Christi, Amarillo, Lubbock, Tyler, and Midland. He caused a stir when he took the four GOP candidates for lieutenant governor to task for comments about undocumented immigrants, saying he was "troubled by the tone" of debate remarks. He urged them to "acknowledge the humanity of a hardworking and productive people." Does he mean amnesty?

While liberals and the mainstream media across the nation are attacking Tea Party and other grassroots conservatives, in Texas, it appears GOP leaders are using the Latino vote and immigration to push back against the conservative grassroots rising tide. The GOP establishment links all Latinos to immigration, as if that is their major concern. They are also trying to scare Anglo Republicans and silence grassroots conservatives.

However, the fact remains that the Tea Party is neither anti-immigrant nor anti-Hispanic. We are anti–illegal immigration, and we want all current immigration laws enforced now. We want the GOP to stop playing race/ethnic politics like the Democrats do and to stop attacking their strongest supporters, conservative grassroots activists.

We want the Texas GOP to understand that Hispanics/Latinos care more about the economy and the defense of our nation, including the borders. They should have a message for all Americans and stop pandering to special interests.

The GOP should blame Democrats and President Obama for the current immigration problems and not the Tea Party and grassroots conservatives.

Finally Texas Republican leaders should stand on the principle of law rather than play race politics.

The Texas GOP should understand that the majority of Hispanics who vote Republican are grassroots conservatives who want stronger enforcement of immigration laws and who are secure in being Americans first. The tough immigration talk doesn't offend them.

Instead of warning Anglo Republicans about losing the Hispanic vote, I will warn them about losing the grassroots conservative vote. That's why the GOP has lost the last two presidential elections.

Texas State Senator Menendez Misses the Mark on Police Interaction Legislation

Law Enforcement and Civil Rights

Democrat Texas state senator Jose Menendez is proposing state legislation that would teach young people how to interact with police officers. Menendez cites the number of shootings of blacks and Latinos by police as the reason for the proposed legislation.

However, rather than grow government with another social program, why doesn't Menendez and all the other concerned politicians speak directly to young people, particularly young minority men, about proper civil behavior?

A pop-thug culture or gangsta behavior is prevalent among minority young men today. Wearing baggy pants, acting tough, swearing, and other forms of antisocial behavior are common.

Rap music, besides often being vulgar, also sometimes glorifies disrespect and even violence against police and other authority. Last year, Hollywood also applauded a movie, *Straight Outta Compton*, which glorified antisocial, anti–law enforcement behavior.

Menendez also ignores the fact that many more minority young people are murdered by other minority young people than the police. Rather than teaching young minority people how to interact with law enforcement, he should teach them how to interact with each other at school, at parties, and in society in general.

Behavior determines life's outcomes. Good behavior leads to good things; bad behavior does not. If State Senator Menendez really wants to help young people, he should preach respectful behavior toward the police and one another and in general. We should teach all young people that "life is not fair" and only the Golden Rule can make it tolerable.

Unfortunately this proposed legislation seems to be more about another minority politician trying to grandstand, pontificate, and play the race card in a different way rather than address the root cause of a problem. We don't need another government program that addresses bad behavior, but in reality excuses or rewards it. We need:

1. parents to teach good civil behavior to their children,
2. community leaders and politicians who preach and emphasize to young people the benefits of good personal behavior,
3. young people to see and understand the consequences of antisocial behavior, and
4. to counter the pop-thug culture that influences (confuses) the minds of young people.

If Texas state senator Jose Menendez is sincere about his desire to address police shootings, he should preach against the culture of violence among minority young men, which causes more deaths than police shootings. Stop the political grandstanding and teach all young people to change bad behavior.

Congressman Joaquin Castro: One of the Most Ineffective Members of Congress

Hispanic Politics

Now that the smoke has cleared a little from the March 1 political primaries, many are scratching their heads about some local incumbents who seem to skate along unscathed by criticism or facts. Among those unchallenged and unscathed is Congressman Joaquin Castro (D-Texas-20) from San Antonio.

According to a GovTrack, InsideGov report in the August 2015 publication of *Business2Community*, Castro is considered one of the least effective members of Congress, yet he seems to get elected regularly without much of a challenge. The local liberal *San Antonio Express-News* avoids criticizing him, while supposed patriotic organizations like veterans' groups also avoid confronting him even when Castro votes to reduce the defense budget or supports the Pentagon's priority to fight climate change instead of ISIS and when Obama reduces veterans' benefits in favor of illegal aliens.

The questions we should ask are: Why isn't Castro held responsible by people in his district? Is the Democrat political establishment that strong in his district, and is local tyranny so entrenched that this ineffective scoundrel goes challenged? Also where are the local GOP and Tea Party to hold him accountable, and why can't they seem to find a challenger?

I wrote a critical opinion piece as "El Conservador" about the Castro twins in 2011, and certain Bexar County GOP leaders were upset because I was going to "stir up the Democrats." Say what?

Congressman Joaquin Castro and his brother, Julian, the former San Antonio mayor and former HUD secretary, are products of liberal elitism. They went to Stanford and Harvard because of affirmative action, not true academic competition. They have been politically promoted because they are Hispanic rather than having achieved real accomplishments.

Voters in Texas Congressional District 20 should analyze Representative Castro's position on issues and his accomplishments and hold him responsible. They will soon realize that Castro follows the liberal ideology of leftist Democrats rather than the will of the majority of Texans. Voters need to remember that the defense of freedom and liberty starts in your backyard.

Race Relations and Law Enforcement

Race and Politics

The men and women of law enforcement are under constant attack. Within a twenty-four-hour period, one officer was lost to an apparent suicide (the third in eighteen months), while another was shot in a road rage incident. Law enforcement in 2016's America, thanks to progressive-liberal Democrats and cowardly Republicans, has become a lawless, amoral society. And law enforcement is expected to control and rein in behavior.

In San Antonio, police and firefighter work is compared shamefully to other bureaucratic paper-pushing government work. At the national level, the federal Border Patrol agents are told to stand down and allow the illegal entry of foreigners into America. And of course the US military is subject to cuts in pay and equipment while they have to endure social engineering experiments.

In 2009, Barak Obama announced he would fundamentally change America with an activist government. His policies and federal agencies have impacted state and local government policies from climate change to gender-neutral bathrooms, all while shaming and cutting law enforcement and the military.

As a constitutional conservative, I feel the only role of government (whether federal, state, or local) is defined in the preamble to the US

Constitution, which is to "establish justice, insure domestic tranquility, provide for the common defense, promote the general welfare."

A nation or society without justice is a tyranny. The Constitution, as well as state constitutions and local charters, provides rules that governments are supposed to follow. People are supposed to be taught morality and proper behavior by their parents and in their family. Let's say that the apple never falls far from the tree.

In order to ensure domestic tranquility, we need a government that implements laws fairly and people who behave in a proper manner. Again, the personal behavior of individuals is a factor because if people don't have a moral code to proper behavior, then someone will step in to monitor and/or control his or her behavior.

All nations must provide for their people's common defense; otherwise they are at the mercy of foreign enemies. The American military and the state and local militia carry out the role of defending home and country. Ordinary citizens are supposed to "provide for the common defense" because the nation belongs to the people and the people are supposed to defend it. It's not the government's military or militia.

Finally, the most debatable role of government is to "promote for the general welfare." The word *promote* is very different from *establish*, *insure*, and *provide*. The general welfare of society and individuals is dependent on behavior and/or morality.

We can promote welfare by encouraging private and personal charity, which again depends on a moral code. Charity comes from the heart, while government welfare comes from forced taxation. Government welfare does not help create a peaceful society.

And we return to the distrust and disrespect exhibited toward law enforcement and the military. It appears America has become a society dominated by insecure people who want government to provide for their general welfare but only promote or encourage justice, domestic tranquility, and common defense.

It has been said that people should hold good principles and be allowed to govern themselves to learn from the consequences. The Constitution is meant to control government but allow secure and moral people to be free. It is not the role of law enforcement to control children (or adults) of any race who are not taught morality, respect, and self-control.

Race and Local Tyranny: Texas State Senator Uresti Indicted

Race and Local Politics

In yet another case of political corruption in south Texas involving a Hispanic Democrat, a federal grand jury indicted a member of a prominent politically connected family.

On Tuesday, May 16, a federal grand jury unsealed two separate indictments against Texas state senator Carlos Uresti of San Antonio, accusing him of multiple criminal acts and financial conspiracies. The charges range from wire fraud to bribery to money laundering, and they could bring a maximum combined sentence of more than 180 years for Uresti.

The first indictment alleges Uresti and his business partners from Four Winds created an investment Ponzi scheme to market fracking sand. Part of the scheme involved them soliciting investors, beginning in 2013, by making false statements and then using money from later investors for personal expenses and payment of earlier investors, according to indictment paperwork.

A second indictment alleges that over the course of ten years Uresti and Vernon Farthing of Lubbock conspired to accept bribes to secure a Reeves County Correctional Center medical services contract for Farthing's company specializing in providing medical services to inmates. Reeves County judge Jimmy Galindo reportedly signed the contract, agreeing to pay Farthing's company a fee per inmate per day.

The indictment further alleges that Farthing paid Uresti $10,000 per month to act as a marketing consultant and that Uresti split that sum with Galindo and others for securing the contract. Bribes (*la mordida*) or "pay for play" are very common in south Texas communities.

Upon conviction of the charges contained in this indictment, Uresti and Farthing face up to five years in federal prison for conspiracy to commit bribery and up to twenty years in federal prison for conspiracy to commit money laundering.

Uresti is part of a politically powerful family in San Antonio / Bexar County that includes Albert Uresti, the Bexar County tax assessor, and Tomas Uresti, Texas state representative for district number 118 in San Antonio.

This makes yet another arrest of a high-ranking Hispanic Democrat in south Texas. Will Republicans and conservatives ever be able to take advantage if these political scandals create a two-party system, particularly in Hispanic communities in south Texas? Stay tuned.

August 12, 2017

Selective Condemnation of Violence in Charlottesville

Race and Politics

The media, Democrats, and some Republicans have been quick to condemn the right, conservatives, whites, males, and Trump over the violence that occurred in Charlottesville, Virginia, on Saturday, August 12, 2017. But it is disingenuous to be selective in any condemnation, and we should review some facts over the past few weeks to recognize that the mainstream media, Democrats, and some Republicans are being selective in their comments about racial bias and violence.

On Sunday, July 31, 2017, the Pod Save America podcast interviewed MSNBC host Joy Reid, who argued the Democratic Party should not try to win over white working-class Donald Trump voters. California Democratic representative Maxine Waters wouldn't rule out the concept of an all-black political party when asked about it on Monday, August 7, 2017. Both Reid and Waters are black females, and for some reason, their comments are not widely condemned or criticized.

In the meantime, politicians or the mainstream media has never truly confronted Black Lives Matter, even though they have threatened and disrupted society and even encouraged the murder of police officers.

Liberalism, militant diversity, and just plain anti-Americanism have caused this great national and social divide, which is leading to violence. Instead of emphasizing Americans' commonalities such as country, history, and cultural integration and assimilation, the left has divided us and emphasized those differences to separate society and the nation.

Unfortunately political correctness and affirmative action politics have allowed one-sided racism and sexism to become acceptable. Minority racism and female sexism get overlooked because minorities and women are the victims. This political correctness has caused deep division and resentment among most of America's silent majority.

Whether whites, blacks, Latinos, LGBT, or others cause the violence, all violence must be condemned. The violence in Charlottesville should be condemned, but so should the black-on-black violence in Chicago, Atlanta, and elsewhere by all politicians and the liberal media.

Selective outrage is phony, and it is interesting that no politicians condemned the leftist Antifa protestors who were also involved in the violence in Charlottesville. The media, Democrats, and Republicans should stop pandering to political correctness and condemn all violence by all people.

In a society where people have self-serving ethics and an adjustable morality, a simple common standard for the rule of law and justice for all citizens becomes difficult. The great question of our time is whether or not America can again become "one nation under God, with liberty and justice for all."

Texas's Voting Map Is Struck Down for Now

Civil Rights—Voting Rights

Democrats are using the courts again to keep Latinos and other minorities politically segregated in the name of racial equality. A special federal judicial panel in the US District Court for the Western District of Texas ruled on Thursday that the redistricting plan adopted by the Texas legislature deliberately diminishes the influence of the growing Latino voting population.

US district judges Xavier Rodriguez (a Democrat appointed by George W. Bush) and Orlando Garcia (another Democrat nominated by Bill Clinton) found that the map was drawn in order to protect incumbent Republican candidates because it did not create any new minority opportunity districts or enhance minority voting strength. Judge Jerry Smith, a Republican, dissented.

While Rodriguez and Garcia may claim the redrawn boundaries fragmented Latino populations into multiple districts and reduced their overall voting power, the real goal by the groups that brought the suit is to create districts that are minority dominant so they can win. LULAC, MALDEF, NAACP, and other racial-oriented groups want to resegregate and politically isolate Latinos and blacks into separate districts where race politics can be easily played.

Social, economic, and political integration happen when people are given the freedom to move around and to develop their own future.

According to Democrats, particularly insecure minority Democrat politicians, protecting their constituents is very important, including keeping them segregated from dangerous ideas like small government, personal freedoms and responsibilities, and lower taxes. These protective politicians are actually controlling political bosses.

Political bosses like Boss Tweed in New York and George and Archer Parr in south Texas used this formula to stay in power in the past. They controlled their voters by controlling people economically and by closely monitoring the votes while pandering to their race, ethnicity, and national origin.

The irony of this case is that voting districts should be drawn up without the consideration of race. Yet LULAC and others are demanding that very approach be taken. They want a racist approach to redrawing the districts.

This case is another example of reverse discrimination that Democrats are using to maintain political control over minorities. They are demanding minority voters be segregated. All minorities should be encouraged to integrate, whether socially or politically. They should be encouraged to become part of mainstream America.

We have often seen how Democrats use the race card when logic and facts fail. This is yet another case, and liberal Hispanic judges are going along with the game plan.

The US Supreme Court must strike down this case because

1. it is the right of states to draw up the districts;
2. the Texas legislature, which drew the districts, is a reflection of all the voters of the state, both minority and nonminority;
3. race was not a consideration in the redrawing of the districts; and

4. it is racial discrimination to segregate minorities into minority-dominant districts.

Ultimately an independent and integrated minority voter seems to be the worst nightmare of Democrats.

Texas Voting Districts Upheld

Race and Politics

Conservatives can claim vindication as the Supreme Court reinstated Texas's controversial congressional redistricting maps that were struck down by two lower courts on Tuesday, September 12, 2017, in a 5–4 ruling.

The immediate legal question were two congressional districts belonging to Democrat congressman Lloyd Doggett and Republican congressman Blake Farenthold, which the lower courts said were drawn unconstitutionally. However, the underlying issue was whether or not a duly elected state legislature, representing the will of a majority of voters, could redraw congressional districts in accordance with political parties.

Democrats used the race card to challenge the new districts, claiming it diluted minority voters and thus representation in elected offices. This decision is a blow to the Voting Rights Act, which has been used to force certain states to comply with federal requirements without clear evidence of discrimination. These states are guilty until they can prove their innocence.

The previous lower court rulings showed the political nature of the federal court system today. In April 2017, US district judges Xavier Rodriguez (a Democrat appointed by George W. Bush) and Orlando Garcia (another Democrat nominated by Bill Clinton) found that the map was drawn in order to protect incumbent Republican candidates because it did not create any new minority opportunity districts or enhance minority voting strength. Judge Jerry Smith, a Republican, dissented. Texas, of course, appealed the ruling.

It should be obvious to everyone that the idea of creating minority districts is a racist idea that Democrats use to create a political spoils system for minority politicians. Liberal judges also seem to accept the idea that party equals race, so Democrats are protected while Republicans are punished, all because of the assumption of race equaling party.

The Democrats have lost state houses and governorships because their party message and race-identity politics have failed, and thus they want to use the courts to win representation. Wisconsin has tried to impose a quota system that ensures districts mirror the voter makeup of the state, again assuming that only Democrats represent minority voters and Republicans don't.

Undoubtedly Democrats will continue to try to win elections through liberal activist courts rather than through public debate and elections. The race card is their last resort, and Democrats will use it as they lose state and federal elections.

Politics in Texas and America should be race and gender blind, and the only legal consideration in drawing voting districts should be one-man-one-vote. However, Democrats are using the race card as a political and a partisan issue to shamefully equate race with party.

Many Texans of Mexican and African descent are not Democrats, and their voice would be drowned out or ignored if they were constantly placed in heavily Democrat districts only because they were a minority. That flies in the face of civil rights and the Constitution. The Supreme Court has recognized that minorities must not be segregated because race does not equal party.

Another Hispanic Democrat Judge Rules against Texas Voter ID Law

Race and Politics

On Wednesday, August 23, US district judge Nelva Gonzales Ramos, a Hispanic Democrat appointed by Obama, rejected a watered-down version of the voter ID law that Texas Governor Greg Abbott signed earlier this year. Judge Ramos's new ruling came three years after she struck down the earlier version of the law.

Texas Democrats recommended Ramos during the Obama administration for the federal bench in the Southern District of Texas. Republican senators Kay Bailey Hutchison and John Cornyn supported her, and the US Senate confirmed her on August 2, 2011.

The ruling blocked Texas from enforcing its revamped voter ID law, claiming that the Texas state legislature's attempt to loosen the law did not go far enough and still perpetuated discrimination against black and Hispanic voters.

It is difficult not to assume that a Democrat Hispanic judge who believes in affirmative action politics could be objective in this case. In April 2017, US district judges Xavier Rodriguez (a Democrat appointed by George W. Bush) and Orlando Garcia (a Democrat appointed by Bill Clinton) overruled Judge Jerry Smith on the judicial panel, claiming that the map protected incumbent Republican candidates because it did not create any new minority opportunity districts or enhance minority voting strength.

However, the real reason for the lawsuit by liberal Democrat minority groups is to create districts that are minority-dominant so they can win. LULAC, MALDEF, NAACP, and other racial-oriented groups want to resegregate and politically isolate Latinos and blacks into separate districts where race politics can be easily played.

Instead of integrating minorities, Democrats want to protect their constituents by keeping them segregated under the thumbs of political bosses. Boss William Tweed in New York and George and Archer Parr in south Texas controlled their voters economically and closely monitored their votes while pandering to their race, ethnicity, and national origin.

This case is also another example of legal discrimination that Democrats use to maintain political control over minorities. Democrats are demanding minority voters be segregated using race as the basis. Old Democrat segregationists would be proud.

This decision by Judge Ramos is the latest round in a yearlong court battle over the state's voter ID rules. Texas could be forced to undergo federal oversight of its election procedures since the state is considered guilty until it proves its innocence under the Voting Rights Act.

Ultimately the US Supreme Court should strike down this case because

1.   it is the right of states to draw up the districts;
2.   the Texas legislature, which drew the districts, is a reflection of all the voters of the state, both minority and nonminority;
3.   race was not a consideration in the redrawing of the districts;
4.   states should not have to prove their innocence—rather the plaintiff should prove a state's guilt; and
5.   it is racial discrimination to segregate minorities into minority-dominant districts.

It continues to appear that an independent and integrated minority voter is the worst nightmare of Democrats.

PART 3
Grassroots Politics

More Logic and Less Emotionalism

Grassroots Politics

Liberal politicians seem to be posturing and bullying at the national, state, and local levels over everything from the national debt to simple political debates on Main Street. In every case, the debates become emotional, and logic and facts are dismissed.

On the national level, President Obama is scaring seniors by saying they may not receive their monthly checks if the debt ceiling is not raised. It was reported that he even stormed out of a meeting with Republicans in a childish tantrum this week when discussing the topic.

Instead of scaring seniors, why not threaten the unions at Chrysler with withholding further federal financial support until they give up their perks? Or why not start mandatory drug testing for welfare recipients to remove those who are breaking the law and don't deserve public assistance?

In Austin, liberals tried to scare parents about education cuts with claims that teachers would be fired, classes would be too large, and their children would suffer. However, they never answered the question about how much money is needed to create a straight-A student nor how many A students are created by spending money to update buildings and hire more administrators.

Liberals forget that you can lead a horse to water, but you can't force it to drink. You can place a child in an academic environment, but you

91

can't force him or her to learn. Learning and the desire to learn start at home with parents. Abe Lincoln and Benito Juarez did not have counselors or modern buildings, but they did have a desire to learn.

At the local level, desperate liberals know they are losing political battles because their arguments lack logic, truth, and wisdom. They charge about threatening anyone and everyone who disagrees with lawsuits.

If they were the local party leaders in the old Soviet Union, they would have dissenters arrested and reeducated. Instead they turn to lawsuits such as the recent one against Medina Valley High in Castroville, Texas, aimed to stop a student's right to say God at the graduation ceremony.

Liberals should read the Constitution and the Bible to understand the law of the land and the rules of a moral society. America's Founding Fathers believed in personal freedom and responsibility, but in limited government. Personal and economic freedom and liberty are the true foundations of a free and civil society.

Liberals should stop scaring and bullying people. Rather they should encourage them to be personally responsible for their actions. Maybe that way we would not need the multitude of government programs that have caused our national debt.

I Am a Hobbit

Grassroots Politics

As a grassroots constitutional conservative, or Tea Party supporter, I have been called a racist, an extremist, and now a "hobbit." On the same day the Speaker of the House John Boehner (R-Ohio) demanded that conservative representatives "get in line" and support his increased debt ceiling, Senator John McCain (R-Arizona) called the Tea Party activists who opposed that legislative action "hobbits."

It's sad when elected leaders who are supposed to represent your political views and who are in leadership positions because of your efforts turn on you. Just as little Bilbo Baggins endured against great odds on his mission and quest, it appears the Tea Party supporters are on a similar mission and quest. We are common ordinary citizens, doing an uncommon thing.

We want the federal government to stop spending and borrowing and going into deeper debt. We want government to be local such as "we the people" rather than to be regulated by bureaucrats who are not accountable to the people. We want local decisions to local issues. We want personal economic freedom and responsibility. We want a strong defense of our nation at the border and abroad. We want protection of individual rights and liberties while promoting personal responsibility, morality, and religious expression. We want a strict adherence to the Constitution and the rule of law. And most of all, we want limited government, sound fiscal policies, and free enterprise.

We know that budgets do not come from the White House, as President Obama demands. They come from Congress and the Democrats who have controlled Congress since January 2007. Democrats had to contend with President George W. Bush in 2007, which caused them to compromise on spending.

However, in fiscal year 2009, Representative Nancy Pelosi and Senator Harry Reid bypassed Bush entirely, passing continuing resolutions to keep government running until President Obama took office. With the House, the Senate, and the White House under their control, they passed a massive omnibus spending bill to complete the fiscal year 2009 budgets.

Obama himself was a member of that Congress that passed all of these massive spending bills, and he signed the omnibus bill as president to complete fiscal year 2009. The total debt increased from $11.9 trillion in fiscal year 2009 to $13.8 trillion in fiscal year 2010 and $15.1 trillion in fiscal year 2011.

The political groundswell that swept Boehner into power as speaker and enhanced McCain's are the hobbits they are disparaging. These hobbits are "we the people" who they are supposed to hear and serve.

What can citizens do when their elected representatives cease to represent and follow their own agenda? What can citizens do when their representatives ridicule them?

If I am a hobbit, then Modor should watch out because neither I nor my fellowship are going away. This is a government of the people, for the people, and by the people, and people will be heard.

The Need for Two Parties in South Texas

Grassroots Politics

For almost forty-five years, south Texas has received billions of dollars in antipoverty government programs. But after all that time and money, it continues to be one of the poorest regions in the nation. In this political season, we should ask if poverty in south Texas is a result of culture, politics, or both, and what is the solution?

The late former US congressman and HUD secretary, Jack Kemp, used to say that the second phase of the civil rights movement for minorities had to be economic freedom. In other words, minorities need to stop worrying about sitting at the front of the bus and concentrate on buying the bus company. Minorities need to learn how to be capitalists so they can partake in the American dream. However, the challenge to minorities, specifically to Mexican Americans in south Texas, is how to overcome culture and politics.

Anthropologist Oscar Lewis argued that the poor do not simply lack resources. They also have a unique value system that often traps them in poverty. Children learn from adults, and they are socialized into behaviors and attitudes that perpetuate their inability to escape the underclass. For example, teens who drop out of school or have children out of wedlock have become a norm in society, yet both actions usually doom the person to a life of poverty.

Very few politicians or community leaders speak out about personal behavior, but instead they choose to demand more government programs that enable or support the underclass values. That leads us to the political issue.

The politics of the patron system or political bosses in south Texas is well documented. They were the few who wanted to control the local economy and political life. Like Boss Tweed of New York, the Parrs of Duval County were famous for saying, "I take care of my people." Today, social welfare programs have become the mechanism through which politicians control their people. The people vote for politicians who provide the social welfare programs that enable and support the underclass values and behavior.

And so after two generations, after the War on Poverty, after the Chicano movement, and after billions of dollars in government grants, south Texas continues to be poor. Whether liberals want to admit it or not, the facts speak for themselves.

South Texas continues with a one-party system that is controlled by the children of old political bosses who now salivate at the idea of the new oil and energy boom. They want to control the local economy by controlling the local politicians. In turn the politicians will guarantee the continued funding of social welfare programs to "take care of their people."

South Texas needs a two-party system because, when politicians compete with ideas, free enterprise will follow, the economy will grow, and people can move themselves out of poverty. Remember, an economically independent citizen/voter is a political boss's worst nightmare.

What Is an Effective Ground Game?

Grassroots Politics

Since the November elections, my opinion has been asked several times as to what Republicans and conservatives need to do to win local elections. I always reply that both need an "effective ground game." Unfortunately I am often met with blank stares. And so let me explain what I mean by an effective ground game.

First, there is the deep and wide ideological divide that exists between mainstream Republicans and conservatives. Even conservatives are divided between fiscal conservatives, Christian conservatives, and libertarians. Each group is ready to fight for their principles, and the word *compromise* is rarely used. Meanwhile, one of the most popular political motto the left has is, "By any means necessary." If Republicans and conservatives want to win, they must be willing to work together.

The second issue is the message. The left, with the help of the mainstream media, has been successful in painting Republicans and conservatives as out of touch with most Americans. Republicans and conservatives need to show how their solutions to local issues are better than the liberal ones. People understand local issues and solutions better than the ideological battles in DC.

Republicans and conservatives depend on talk radio or Fox News for their messaging system. However, the mainstream media and many small local media outlets have a heavy liberal slant. If people in Third

World countries can use various forms of electronic media to help their revolutions, certainly the conservatives and Republicans can use them to inform and educate each other about local issues and candidates.

Finally, there is the role of party precinct chairs and grassroots leaders. Contrary to what liberals believe, political power starts at the local level with local voters. Unfortunately most citizens focus on national issues more than local ones. They forget that local governments and school districts have grown dependent on federal money, which feeds the deficit. What if local governments and school districts had elected officials who stopped depending on federal money? This idea is lost on conservative and Republican voters.

Liberals also have unions, leftist activists, civil rights groups, and many people who are constantly—yes, constantly—in front of local voters. They add a personal touch to voters, and there is no conservative counterpart.

Precinct chairs and local grassroots leaders are the key to the ground game. Many people do not know who their GOP precinct chairs are, and many grassroots leaders lead no one but themselves. Unless these folks are active in their neighborhood and community, the liberals' personal touch will always win out. Precinct chairs and grassroots leaders can recruit new voters, including Hispanics, and get out the vote if they are active.

Unless Republicans and conservatives work together, communicate an effective message on local issues, and get their local followers to be active, they will lose at the national level because they will lose at the local level. It's that simple.

August 28, 2013

Fast-Food Workers Strike for Higher Wages

Unions, Economics, and Grassroots Politics

On Thursday, August 29, 2013, fast-food workers in many American cities are planning to strike for higher wages. The liberal Service Employees International Union (SEIU) support them. In typical liberal fashion, the SEIU is deceiving employees with half-truths while ignoring the realities of life and America.

Most people feel everyone is equal and should be paid equally. They are quick to accept the idea that all people should have a living wage and dignity at work. Those assumptions are great ideas but not factual.

First, in real life we are not created equal except before the law. Some people are short and others tall. A few are heavy. (Can I say "fat" anymore?) Several are thin. Many are old, and a few are young. Some are educated and trained. Others are not. Some are motivated. And others are not so much.

Second, the choices we make influence our lives. Bad choices and decisions lead in one direction and good ones in another. In America, people usually end up in a given socioeconomic status because of their choices in life, not because some Supreme Power dictates it. Tomorrow, the rich can become poor and the poor can become rich, if they make the right choices.

Third, America's society and economy is not static and rigid where a person is doomed to labor in the class into which he or she was born.

This is another lie that leftists try to sell. America has been the land of opportunity because people have always been able to come here and fulfill their dream with ambition, vision, and work.

Fourth, American fast-food workers are not tied to their jobs like serfs or slaves. They can quit and search for better-paying jobs. The fast-food industry has always been a starter or temporary job industry for people because of its wages. I would seriously question any person who wants to make cooking and serving burgers at McDonald's a life career.

Finally, the free market is the best way to allow an economy to grow and expand and thus create a better society. A growing and expanding economy allows for jobs, high-paying and starter/temporary ones, to be created. A free market economy will have many jobs where employers and employees can compete for each other. Employers will use wages to entice workers, who will use their abilities to merit wages.

But liberals, with the help and support of the Obama administration, have pushed class warfare into yet another facet of the American economy. It's not enough that Obama has created a divisive society based on race and gender or a political atmosphere that ignores the US Constitution. Now he and his liberal friends want to undermine the economy with class warfare.

The question is whether business leaders, particularly small business leaders, and politicians will stand up to this socialist charade. We cannot let the economic model that made America the greatest nation on earth fall victim to liberals who exploit socially insecure people with half-truths. If you don't like your current job, find another but don't expect the government or someone else to change things for you.

Local Tyranny and Supporting First Responders

Grassroots and Local Politics

The level of ignorance by the San Antonio establishment (political, business, and even social elite) never ceases to amaze. For example, they misunderstand how much the grassroots conservatives and the San Antonio firefighters and police officers have in common. Their arrogance seems to be similar to that of Obama and liberals at a national level regarding the defense of the nation.

Most of the firefighters and police have conservative values similar to those espoused by the Tea Party movement. Many have military backgrounds, which breeds patriotism. Also because they truly place themselves in harm's way on a daily basis, most are spiritual, if not religious. Both of these values are a core part of conservatism.

Firefighters and police officers also see the failures and abuses of big government on a daily basis. They see the breakdown of the family, people who abuse the welfare system, and persons who have no regard for the law because they feel entitled (both rich and poor). They also see the truly needy who fall through the bureaucratic cracks. These are all core concerns of grassroots conservatives.

These first responders in our community carry out core government responsibilities. Their role is similar to that of our national military and Border Patrol. One protects our nation and its borders; the other protects our communities and each person.

Unfortunately the establishment in San Antonio seems to be viewing our first responders in the same manner as Obama is perceiving our military and Border Patrol. The city, supported by the San Antonio Chamber, wants to classify them the same as any municipal bureaucrat and cut back on their benefits and personnel to save money. That reason is as ironic as it is cynical.

City Manager Sheryl Sculley, working on behalf of the establishment and not the taxpayer/citizen, is willing to help fund projects and programs that are duplicated by federal and state programs, like job training programs and pre-K / day care. She is also willing to support foolish expensive and unnecessary projects like streetcars for downtown, all in the name of economic development.

If Sculley, the city council, and their cronies at the Chamber wanted to truly save taxpayers' money, they would listen to grassroots conservatives. They should cut the municipal government's waste and duplication.

The San Antonio establishment believes in big government, and big business lives off big government's contracts. However, they don't want to hear from the little people who pay the bills. In order to save their streetcars project, Sculley and the city have started a public relations campaign funded by big businesses to convince taxpayers that the police and firefighters are greedy for challenging the streetcars.

Just like Obama has made the nation vulnerable by shrinking the military, the local establishment is expanding their projects for downtown developers and tourists, all at the expense of our public safety.

The time has come for the citizens of San Antonio to change the political landscape and attitude at city hall. It's time for citizens/taxpayers to determine the city's destiny since we pay the bills. Grassroots conservatives and first responders should stand together.

Let's put public safety first.

The Democratic Party Establishment

Grassroots Politics and the Democratic Party

Bernie Sanders won the Wisconsin Democratic primary, beating Hillary Clinton on Tuesday night, and it raises several questions that the mainstream media and most political pundits seem to be ignoring about the Democrats and their two candidates.

For example, what will the Sanders supporters do when Hillary gets the nomination in spite of all of his primary victories because of the superdelegates? It is obvious the superdelegate system has stacked the deck against anyone who the grown-ups in the Democratic Party don't want, and the superdelegates want Hillary Clinton. Are the Bernie supporters so politically immature and naive, so blinded by anti-Republican and anticonservative hate, that they'll follow Hillary and the Democrat bosses anyway? Will they ignore the fact that the fix is in, no matter how many primaries Bernie wins?

Secondly, there has been a lot of talk, particularly in Texas and California, about a Latino/Hispanic running mate for Hillary to reflect the future of the party and the nation. However, it appears that young whites aren't following that game plan and are continuing to support Sanders in large numbers while Hispanics and blacks line up behind Clinton. What happens when Sanders gets to the Democratic convention with an almost equal amount of delegates to Clinton's? Will Sanders be picked as the running mate over someone like Julian Castro? Will the Democrat seek to unify the party with Sanders, or will they continue to play the race/gender card and ignore the old white man?

If at any time in history the Democratic Party has shown itself to be the party of race, gender, income, age, and other special interests, it is in 2016. The final question is "Can a party that specializes in division and diversity be unified, or is the hatred and fear—yes, hatred and fear—of conservatives and Republicans enough to unify Bernie Sanders and Hillary Clinton supporters?"

And, yes, the same thing can be said about Republicans if and when they get to their convention and neither Ted Cruz nor Donald Trump is nominated. Both Cruz and Trump are anti-GOP establishment candidates. What will the Cruz and Trump supporters do if they sense a rigged convention? Maybe we are living in a time when establishments really know what's best for us. Or maybe we are living in a time when the establishment just doesn't care what we think is best for us.

Political leaders seem to have forgotten or ignored that our government grows from the grassroots up, not with omnipotent political bosses, party superdelegates, or any establishment organization.

Astroturf Groups versus Grassroots Groups

Grassroots Politics, Real and Fake

On Thursday night, February 9, nearly a thousand people, most of them Democrats, crashed a town hall meeting in Utah held by Congressman Jason Chaffetz, the Republican chair of the House Oversight Committee. They were upset with Chaffetz about his support of President Trump's agenda and cabinet appointments. The protesters yelled and drowned out the congressman's attempts to respond to questions, a typical leftist Saul Alinsky tactic. They talk or scream, and you listen.

This protest was part of other protests across the nation as the Democrats try to create their Tea Party movement. Just as the grassroots constitutional conservatives organized in 2009 and helped the GOP win first the House, then the Senate, most of the state governorships, and now the White House, the Democrats now want to copy the movement and its success.

However, the Democrats miss the point. The grassroots constitutional conservative movement is a *grassroots* movement born among the people, not in a backroom political strategy meeting by a top-down party leadership. The Democrats can't seem to understand the concept of free people acting on their own behalf rather than depending on political bosses to tell them what to do.

Just like Pharaoh's magicians who tried to copy Moses when he used God's power to turn his staff into a snake, leftists are trying to copy the conservative constitutional grassroots movement with one that is not rooted in the people.

What is also curious is how the liberal media has been quick to embrace, promote, and cover the leftist protests. The media has consistently ignored or downplayed conservative events and gatherings, yet now they show great interest in the leftists' rallies, protests, and meetings. We might say it's a fake movement (Astroturf) for fake news.

The lesson is simple. The defense of freedom and liberty starts in your backyard with you, not with a political boss.

Globalism versus Local Governance

Grassroots and Globalists

In matters of local and state elections, are your candidates globalists or localists? A globalist is someone who places the interests of the entire world above those of individual nations or citizens. A localist is someone who places his or her interests on what is happening in his or her home and community.

Globalists feel it is important to compete in the world market by allowing businesses to sell abroad; however, the trade-off is that cheap foreign goods are allowed to be sold locally. This hurts local small businesses that cannot compete with cheap foreign goods.

Globalists also feel societies must be sensitive to foreign cultures and people because we are all one world. Local and state policies are designed to accommodate foreigners, in many cases at the expense of local citizens. For example, many local citizens are turned down for jobs because they don't speak a certain language.

The localist wants to serve the local community and its residents first and foremost. They want to pave the neighborhood streets and sidewalks to keep the citizens safe and to provide an economic environment that provides opportunities for local entrepreneurs to grow and develop.

State and local governments are filled with elected officials who are globalists, and Bexar County judge Nelson Wolff and San Antonio mayor Ivy Taylor are good examples. Both, as the county's and city's high-ranking elected officials, want to create a global city. In order to do that, they and the San Antonio Chamber say there must be public investment. But how much local investment (government spending and debt) is necessary to satisfy global interests, and how much do local interests have to suffer?

For example, according to 2015 Texas comptroller figures, Bexar County's tax supported debt was $1.43 billion and San Antonio's was $1.49 billion. Plus San Antonio has an additional revenue supported debt of $8.9 billion. Citizens in San Antonio ask, "Where did that money go?" when they are asked to vote on a proposed 2017 $500 million municipal bond and when they hear globalist officials talk about making the county and city a global community.

The preamble to the Constitution clearly outlines the role of the federal government and should be the blueprint for state and local governments. It establishes justice through the rule of law and the process of a representative government. It ensures domestic tranquility by allowing citizens to protect themselves, and to be protected by local public safety officials. It provides for the local common defense against lawlessness and crime. It promotes, not assures or guarantees, the general welfare. This is how it secures the blessings of liberty for the individual citizen.

The priority of the federal, state, and local governments in Texas and the United States should be the local citizen, not the world. Citizens should understand that defense of freedom and liberty starts in their backyard, not in the rest of the world.

The Latest in South Texas Political Corruption

Local Tyranny

This morning, Wednesday, April 26, the FBI carried out searches across the state as part of a public corruption probe centered on Laredo and Webb County. The investigation appears to focus on Dannembaum Engineering, a firm with offices in several Texas cities that has taken on high-profile contracts in Laredo. The buildings searched included Laredo City Hall, the City Hall Annex, the Public Works Department, the offices of Webb County Precinct Four Commissioner, Jaime Canales, and the offices of Dannenbaum Engineering in Laredo, San Antonio, Houston, and McAllen.

Two years ago, in April 2015, FBI and Internal Revenue Service agents arrested Val Verde County (Del Rio) Precinct One Commissioner Ramiro Ramon, sixty-two. He was charged in a twenty-three-count indictment with bribery, theft of honest service, wire fraud, false statements on tax returns, and violation of the travel act. He was charged with taking bribes from a San Antonio developer and a group of New Braunfels business owners, according to federal prosecutors in Del Rio.

Yesterday, Thursday, April 27, 2017, the former Val Verde County commissioner pleaded guilty Thursday to charges that he underreported his total income on three separate federal income tax returns, the US Attorney's Office for the Western District of Texas said.

In the past five years, almost fifty public officials ranging from sheriffs and district attorneys to mayors, school boards, city council members, and county commissioners have been arrested in south Texas from Del Rio to Brownsville. These investigations and arrests have exposed the deep-rooted establishments or political machines that control local politics in south Texas communities. A common theme is how elected officials award contracts, while businesses that get the contracts turn around and support those elected officials with campaign funds to be reelected.

While the arrests provide a glimmer of hope to local citizens and taxpayers, it is curious how the state GOP has not been able to take advantage of the many cases. In the meantime, other grassroots activists can look for hope in addressing the corruption in their local governments, like in San Antonio.

Listen Up, GOP!

Politics and Grassroots Conservatism

There should be a notice to all state and local Republican Party leaders that GOP Party supporters do not exist to serve the will of the party, but rather the party should reflect their politics. If it doesn't, then the party must change or fail.

For example, Texas house speaker Joe Straus (R–San Antonio) and his party supporters have shown an antagonism toward grassroots conservatives by ignoring and dismissing several state legislative bills that were based on the state Republican platform, such as the Privacy Bill. A majority of party activists who were grassroots conservatives crafted the platform.

Texas grassroots conservatives have been loyal to the Republican Party and have given them a political majority in the state government. In fact, they have made it the most Republican state in the union.

Since 1994, a Republican has held every statewide elected office. After the 2010 elections, Republicans held a super-majority of 101 Republican representatives in the 150-member body Texas House of Representatives, but that number has dwindled slightly to 99 out of 150 seats. In the Texas State Senate, Republicans hold twenty of thirty-one seats after the 2014 elections.

At the federal level, the Texas congressional delegation is composed of twenty-four Republicans and twelve Democrats, and both of its US senators, Ted Cruz and Majority Whip John Cornyn, are Republicans.

The last Democratic presidential candidate to carry Texas was Jimmy Carter in 1976.

However, despite all the gains, the Republican Party seems to have failed their supporters. At the state level, Speaker Straus, the third-most powerful Republican in the state, has been an impediment to the conservative legislative agenda. Straus has stated that he does not support the state GOP platform, and he has blocked important conservative legislation.

At the national level, John Cornyn, the senior senator, serves as the Senate majority whip, whose role is to gather votes on major issues. However, Cornyn has failed to gather votes on the repeal of ObamaCare, even though that issue has been the rallying cry for Republicans for the past seven years.

Texas Republicans owe grassroots conservatives for their party's success, and as the late University of Texas football coach Darrell Royal used to say, "You need to dance with who brought you to the dance." Unfortunately some of the Republican elected officials seem to forget who brought them to the dance.

With the Republican Party in control of every major statewide office in Texas and in control of the presidency and congress in DC, failing to deliver on the will of the people who put them in power to represent them is not an option or tolerable.

Republicans in Washington must repeal ObamaCare, and those in Austin must pass legislative bills proposed by Texas Governor Greg Abbott. They should also remove Straus as speaker.

Political power in Texas and America starts at the grassroots, not in DC or Austin, and it is not granted by any government. In a representative form of government, the elected officials should/must reflect the will of voters they represent. Republican leaders and elected officials who do not hear the people should be replaced. Or perhaps the party should be replaced.

August 7, 2017

Gentrification in San Antonio

Grassroots and Local Taxes

Some homeowners south of San Antonio's downtown fear they will lose their homes after becoming aware of the increasing property values in their neighborhood. Apparently the appraisal amounts for several houses along Lone Star Boulevard south of downtown San Antonio have jumped 70 to 90 percent in value in five years.

A WOAI radio news report in 2016 showed the average San Antonio taxpayer owes $3,300 toward the city's long-term debt as the municipal debt balloons. Couple that with school district, college district, health district, county, state, and federal taxes and fees. This municipal money is for the maintenance of basic government services like fire, police, streets, and sidewalks.

But it is also for pet political projects like painting crosswalks rainbow colors, duplicating pre-K school programs, and developing plans for light rail that the taxpayers/voters have repeatedly turned down. Taxpayers have to pay for all of this city spending through taxes and fees. What's interesting is that the same people who claim to support the poor are the ones who have allied themselves with developers to gentrify neighborhoods.

Liberal politicians love to spread the wealth, but somehow they never eradicated poverty while developers who donate to their election seem to prosper. They also seem to concentrate on fixing neighborhoods, but not people's behavior or the life skills that would lift them out of poverty. They never address the culture of poverty, but rather prefer to fix the person's environment.

It is apparent the worth of a parcel of land is greater than the worth of a person to liberals. When a neighborhood is gentrified, the property becomes more valuable, and it generates more revenue through taxes for the government. And liberals control the government and its spending.

It is also interesting how the local news media does not connect the tax-and-spend behavior and consequential raise in property taxes directly to specific frivolous and unnecessary projects like light rail, painting crosswalks, statues, and public toilets.

San Antonio recently elected the most liberal mayor and city council in its history. Their agenda will be more tax-and-spend with a focus on global issues like tying local transportation solutions to global climate change and funding the defense of illegal aliens with city money.

Private property ownership, whether it is a shack or a mansion, is what has made America great because "a man's home is his castle." Any public policy that undermines or hinders a citizen's ability's to create personal wealth by owning private property is un-American.

It is sad that the San Antonio city council districts that suffer or are targeted for gentrification—excuse me, "redevelopment"—consistently vote for some of the most liberal public officials in the city, county, and state. Taxpayers/voters need to become aware that these officials are not serving their interest.

Wake up, San Antonio! The defense of freedom, liberty, and property rights starts in your backyard with your vote. Conservative advocacy groups should focus on local neighborhood issues like the rise in local taxes to hold elected officials or city hall accountable or to replace them.

Straus and the South Texas Hispanic Democrat Connection

Grassroots Politics

While the Democratic Party strongholds in south Texas, including San Antonio, Laredo, Valverde County, and the Rio Grande Valley, have been racked with political scandals, the Republican Party seems to have failed to take advantage of those problems to grow the GOP in the region. Why?

Let's remember that Straus won the speakership in 2009 by first reaching out to the Democrats for their support. Once he had their block of votes, he convinced enough Republicans to gain the magic seventy-six number to the speaker position. Once he had the votes needed, other Republicans had to play politics and fall in line. But Straus never forgot his Hispanic Democrat friends in south Texas who supported him. He appointed Democrats to committee chairs, effectively giving power to stop any legislation.

Equally important, he discouraged or ignored GOP candidates who challenged his Democrat friends. Thus the GOP failed to take advantage of the hundreds of political scandals in the region. Straus has not rocked the boat for his Democrat friends in Austin or their home districts. It is absolutely shameful that the third-most powerful Republican in the most Republican state in America would turn his back on a region of the state racked with Democrat political scandal for his own political advantage.

Texas has a new conservative, grassroots-oriented state Republican chairman, James Dickey, who respects the will of the Republican delegates by supporting the GOP state platform. Governor Greg Abbott and Lieutenant Governor Dan Patrick likewise are pushing state legislation that is based on the platform because it reflects the will of the people in the party. However, Straus has never supported the platform. He has called the legislative agenda "manure," and he has slowed the legislative process to delay and/or kill bills.

Not only is Straus an impediment to conservative legislation in Texas, he has prevented the growth of the Republican Party in south Texas by refusing to capitalize on the Democratic political scandals in south Texas. This is very ironic since many GOP moderates are always talking about Hispanic outreach.

If the GOP is going to grow in South Texas, Straus needs to get out of the way so that Democrats can be challenged. It's sad that almost a hundred Democratic Party elected officials have been indicted in Texas in a twenty-year span, and no Republicans (if any) have replaced them.

South Texas needs a grassroots conservative revolution that the Republican Party supports. Let freedom ring from the Alamo to the Rio Grande.

The People versus Big Money Lobbyists and the Media

Grassroots Politics and Border Security

While most conservative Americans are focusing on the letdown by the Republican-elected officials in Congress, Texans should not forget the two biggest RINOs that impede the conservative agenda for the most conservative state in the union, Congressman Will Hurd and Texas Speaker Joe Straus. If anyone is going to beat these two powerful politicians who have lots of lobbyists' money, it will require organizing grassroots voters and getting them to the polls.

Hurd is promoting himself with the media's help. CNN (fake news) proudly announced on July 27, 2017, that Hurd and his moderate friends "want to take control" of the border wall debate with the help of friends from Silicon Valley. Are those the same Silicon Valley friends who support open borders and unrestricted immigration?

According to the report, Hurd wants a high-tech fence on the border. However, a high-tech fence will provide more contracts for Silicon Valley liberals (and contributors to Hurd), but it will be vulnerable because it can shut down if the power grid goes down or if it gangs crash it. We need a high, strong wall backed up by the Border Patrol and the military, if necessary, with updated equipment. Apparently Hurd gets his ideas from his Democrat pals he hangs out with.

Let's remember the recent DC bromance that blossomed when Hurd drove from San Antonio to DC in a car with Democrat Congressman

Beto O'Rourke from El Paso. Hurd announced after the trip that he could work with the Democrats. He then stood with linked arms with Democrats like Joaquin Castro at the border denouncing the proposed wall, while O'Rourke announced he was challenging Senator Ted Cruz for his seat. Also given the Hurd-O'Rourke and Castro bromance, might we expect Democrats to cross over and vote for Hurd in the GOP primary? Could be.

Then there's Speaker Straus. The Texas State Senate and its president, Lieutenant Governor Dan Patrick, have been working at top speed to pass the twenty items on Governor Greg Abbott's agenda for the special legislative session. The chamber approved eighteen bills in just the first week by working late into the night and through the weekend. Much of the agenda Abbott laid out in June aligns with conservative proposals Patrick pushed during the regular session.

The Texas House, on the other hand, is moving at a slower pace, a strategy House Speaker Joe Straus has called "deliberate." This slower pace is nothing more than a deliberate effort to stall the conservative legislative agenda in the state legislature.

It's difficult for conservative Republican voters to be loyal and respect a Republican Party when its leaders like Straus don't respect the party platform and principles that the party faithful crafted at the state GOP party convention. Straus has called the legislative agenda in the special session, which is based on the party platform, "manure."

If anyone is going to beat the two biggest RINOs in Texas, Hurd and Straus, it will have to be by organizing the grassroots voters and getting them to the polls. Hurd and Straus have the liberal mainstream media and big money lobbyists on their side. The media will always side against grassroots conservatives in favor of liberals and moderates, and the lobbyists will provide large amounts of money funding the Hurd and Straus campaigns.

These two election campaigns will literally be "the people" versus "big money lobbyists and the media." The people, the grassroots citizens, should use social media to inform and educate themselves and then get voters to the polls in the primary.

August 30, 2012

Why Hide Your Voting Record?

Politics

Why are some liberal Democrat candidates in south Texas hiding their records this 2012 election season? They seem to be avoiding two things: a public stand on certain issues like abortion and same-sex marriage and/or tying themselves to President Obama and his policies.

Take, for example, State Representative Ryan Guillen (D-Dist.31) from Rio Grande City and State Senator Juan Hinojosa (D-S20) from McAllen. Both Guillen and Hinojosa represent the Eagle Ford area of Texas, yet their voting records reflect an anti-energy attitude. Guillen had legislative ratings of 92 percent in 2009 and 73 percent in 2011 from the Sierra Club. Hinojosa had ratings of 100 percent from the Sierra Club in 2009 and 86 percent for a Lifetime score in 2011 from Environment Texas. They don't mention their ties to anti-energy groups like the Sierra Club. Nor do they say anything about the Democratic Party's and Obama's green agenda.

Republican Ann Matthews of San Antonio is challenging Guillen, and she has stated clearly that she supports the energy industry in south Texas because it brings jobs and economic growth to south Texas. Likewise, Raul Torres, a Republican from Corpus Christi, has taken a pro-energy position as the best solution to the region's unemployment problems and the nation's independence.

Another example is State Senator Pete Gallego, a Democrat from Alpine who is running against U.S. Congressman Francisco "Quico" Canseco. Gallego got a 100 percent rating from the Texas Club in 2009 and 2011. He also was rated at 20 percent on social issues, personal liberties, and property rights from the Libertarian Party during the same period.

Then there is State Representative Joaquin Castro (D–San Antonio) who is running for the 20th US congressional seat vacated by Charles Gonzalez of San Antonio. He received a 100 percent rating from NARAL and the Sierra Club in 2009 and 2011, but he keeps a low profile on that record.

While a majority of Texans supported the voter ID law and reduced state spending, Guillen, Hinojosa, Castro, and Gallego all opposed those bills. They also opposed the redistricting and the sanctuary cities, and they refused to sign the Taxpayer Protection pledge sponsored by Empower Texans.

When will these liberals own up to their voting records? Guillen, Hinojosa, Castro, and Gallego have liberal voting records that are pro-abortion, tax-and-spend, and anti-energy business. They also seem to be keeping a distance from Obama.

The voters deserve to know whom they are electing. These liberals may want to keep a low profile on their record, but isn't that deceiving the voters? The beliefs and positions of these four liberal candidates—Guillen, Hinojosa, Castro, and Gallego—should be brought out into the light of day for all to examine and view. Why are they hiding their records? They should be honest and tell the voters the truth about how they have voted in the past and what they really believe.

Obama's Failed Energy Policy and South Texas

Energy Policy

Since the beginning of the nineteenth century, oil and coal have determined how strong a nation is or isn't. Unfortunately in 2012, the greatest and most progressive nation the world has even known is being starved of energy by its own leader, President Barack Obama.

Gas prices have doubled since Obama took office. According to the GasBuddy gasoline price tracking website, the price of a gallon of regular gas was around $1.79 when Mr. Obama took office. Today the national average is $3.58. The lowest average price in the continental United States is $3.31 in Tulsa, Oklahoma. The highest is $4.14 in Santa Barbara, California. Four-dollar-a-gallon gas has arrived on average throughout California, and a number of other states are headed in that direction. Energy analysts are predicting even higher prices by summer.

As for the coal industry, in 2009, Obama's EPA announced a set of "enhanced coordination procedures" that the EPA said would strengthen the environmental review of pending mining applications and help address a backlog of permit decisions. The procedures became an impediment to the coal industry, which eventually led to the state of West Virginia challenging Obama and the EPA.

In October 2011, a federal district judge ruled that the EPA unlawfully tried to curb coal mining operations. The EPA exceeded its own authority beginning in June 2009 when it set up a new process for issuing clean water permits in an effort to protect mining communities from polluted water, according to a decision by US district judge Reggie Walton. By doing so, it entangled permits necessary to Appalachian coal operators, Walton said.

The reason for Obama's antagonism toward oil and coal has several factors:

1. Obama believes that America's role as a global power—liberals would say bully—is past, and we must share the earth and its resources with the rest of world.
2. He has rabid environmentalists on his side who believe carbon-based energy is destroying the earth.
3. These same environmentalists want Americans to stop being dependent on oil and coal and start looking toward clean energy.

While these ideas are noble, they are not realistic. America needs oil and coal to keep its economy growing and strong. We also need this energy to defend ourselves from our enemies. Canada, a friend and neighbor, has lots of gas and was ready to share it with the United States, but Obama chose to kill the deal.

Closer to home, Obama and his EPA have done everything possible to stop offshore drilling and to scare people about fracking for gas in south Texas's Eagle Ford. And the local Democrats support their party more than the local economy.

Yes, we should look for new future fuels, but we cannot and must not stop drilling and refining oil or mining for coal. America is and can be strong again, but apparently not under Obama. Obama and his supporters have weakened America with a failed, liberal, and unrealistic energy policy. We should remember in November.

Limiting the Government's Power through a Balanced Budget Amendment

Grassroots Politics versus a National Government Power

Our Founding Fathers established the government of the United States on the ideals of personal liberty and freedom from government intervention. However, today many Americans seem to expect the government to intervene and care for most of their needs.

This has caused great debate over the role of government in a citizen's life. Some people want limited government, while others expect the government to protect them from everything from foreign invasions to sugar drinks.

The government provides housing, education, transportation, health care, a military, state/local public safety, unemployment benefits, and Social Security. Taxpayers pay for all of this through federal, state, and local taxes and fees, but it's not enough, and it will never be enough as long as the government continues to grow. But governments cannot afford to take care of every need in a citizen's life. A citizen must have some personal responsibility and provide something to merit assistance.

The war over the role of government is not just a political one but also a cultural one that has implications on the role of government itself. As a constitutional conservative, I believe Americans must learn to be more personally responsible for themselves, and they should expect (want) less involvement from the government in everything from dietary to financial decisions.

The government cannot and should not protect some people from themselves. People grow from personal experiences, and as people grow, so do societies and economies. On the other hand, people who are overprotected never mature socially and become more dependent on external (government) assistance.

A government needs money to operate, and that money comes from the people in the form of taxes and fees. The answer to our huge government and national dependence on government programs is a Balanced Budget Amendment (BBA) to the US Constitution.

Just like the goal in the Revolutionary War was political independence, the new objective should be to keep the federal government from growing larger and getting into financial trouble that cannot be resolved. All political candidates in 2012 should be asked if they support a BBA to separate those who want to serve the nation from those who want political power.

America was born from the ideals of personal freedom, liberty, and responsibility, and there is a never-ending struggle between governments and individuals over power. We cannot surrender our personal responsibilities because the government will assume them and then charge us for being our caretaker.

We must limit government's power by limiting its money with a Balanced Budget Amendment.

Texas versus ObamaCare

ObamaCare

In typical leftist, politically immature behavior, liberals in Texas are screaming and claiming that Texas Governor Rick Perry and other Republican state legislative leaders "want people to die" because they oppose expanding Medicaid under President Obama's health care law. Never mind the facts. It's the emotion that counts for liberals.

Liberals ignore that the Supreme Court has determined that, because of our federalist system of government, states can choose whether or not to allow the federal expansion of Medicaid. Under the Supreme Court's decision last year, Texas has the right to determine whether they want to accept ObamaCare.

Furthermore, liberals ignore the fact that we have a broken health care insurance and payment system that should be addressed, not expanded. Just like the liberal approach to the broken public education system is to spend more money, that's their idea for ObamaCare.

Governor Perry joined the state's GOP senators, Ted Cruz and John Cornyn, and other lawmakers in Austin to reiterate their opposition to ObamaCare and to call for flexibility in how they implement Medicaid, a health entitlement program for the poor that they view as broken.

"Medicaid is a broken system that is failing Texans and overwhelming the state budget," Senator Cornyn said. "The program must be fundamentally reformed, and Texas—not the federal government—is best suited to design a health care program for its poorest and most vulnerable residents."

Governor Perry and others have stated correctly that expanding the federal health care program would make Texas hostage to the federal government. "It would benefit no one in our state to see their taxes skyrocket and our economy crushed as our budget crumbled under the weight of oppressive Medicaid costs," Perry has said.

Another fact the liberals ignore is that Texas had a $25 billion deficit in 2011, but an $8 billion surplus this biennium. That's due to Texas living within its means. Texas lawmakers are considering reducing the deficit by dropping out of Medicaid because it would be such a large, expensive burden.

Medicaid consumes more than 20 percent of the Texas state budget, and ObamaCare will force the state to massively expand our already burdensome Medicaid rolls. Starting in 2014, all states must expand Medicaid to all nonelderly individuals with family incomes below 138 percent of the federal poverty level. ObamaCare will pick up the first three years of benefit costs, but in 2017, states begin to shoulder a larger and larger share of these benefit costs, maxing out at 10 percent by 2020.

However, none of these facts matter to liberals. For them, emotions are everything. Their argument is that Texas is heartless for hurting the poor, and the government must redistribute the wealth, regardless of whether the program actually is working.

Democrats want to take over Texas by 2018, and their emotional arguments favoring the expansion of Medicaid will resonate along with allegations of racism, sexism, and class warfare. But Texans must stand tough and not be frightened by liberal emotionalism.

We should examine the health insurance industry and the cost of insuring high-risk people, not redistributing the wealth of taxpayers under the guise of universal health care.

It's Time to Bring the Trump Populist Revolt Home

Politics and Local Tyranny

Wake up, grassroots patriots! The Trump populist revolution must be brought home to the local governments. Citizens and taxpayers must wrestle local political power away from the establishments that control our local politics and economy for their own agenda. Big business interests control elected officials with campaign contributions and donations to politicians, while the politically correct / social engineering interests strip away our individual liberties and freedoms in the name of fairness and justice (or revenge).

When was the last time a municipal, county, or state official (elected or appointed) met with you personally and asked and acted on your opinion? When was the last time a local or state official stood his or her ground on behalf of your individual rights rather than for the community good?

Then think of the last time a local/state official enacted ordinances or legislation on behalf of a big money contributor or loud politically correct / social engineering group. Think of the last time your tax money was invested for a project that would benefit the community but put you deeper in government debt and doesn't really serve you or your neighborhood. Think of the last time a minority of persons forced changes on the majority in the name of fairness and equality.

Finally, think of the last time the local/state mainstream media wrote articles that supported change and condemned the grassroots opposition as "reactionary" and "obstructionist."

The time has come to challenge the establishments that dominate local governments, those that have placed taxpayers and citizens in additional debt beyond the $20 billion of federal debt. We must challenge the establishments that have created burdensome rules and regulation that stifle the local economy and your personal business development. We must challenge the establishments that serve themselves rather than the public. We must challenge the establishments that curtail personal freedoms and liberties in the name of the greater good. We must not expect the cavalry to arrive in the form of the Trump administration to save us.

Let's start by voting against municipal and school district bonds that create more debt. Let's start by electing local officials who are truly public servants rather than establishment puppets. Let's start by using social media to inform and educate our citizens and taxpayers rather than letting them depend on the local mainstream media.

The US Constitution applies to every citizen in every community, and we must fight and resist when local governments seek to restrict those freedoms. It is time for grassroots patriots to defend our freedoms and liberties in our backyard.

Republicans Can Win in Washington as Long as We Don't Raise Taxes

Grassroots and Taxes

Amid the endless gridlock and internal bickering in Washington, the Republican Congress has a real opportunity to do some good for the American people. Americans want lower taxes and a simpler way to pay them. What we do not want is higher taxes, especially on goods we buy each and every day.

Republican leadership, Speaker Paul Ryan, and House Ways and Means Chairman Kevin Brady are proposing what they call a "Border Adjustment Tax," or as it should be called, the "American Middle-Class Consumer Tax." This new tax would hit small businesses and consumers the hardest, raising the price on everything from food and clothing to gasoline and motor vehicles, all for the benefit of large corporations who already exploit the complicated tax system and pay effectively no taxes at all.

For example, imagine tacking on an extra thirty-five cents a gallon on your next fill-up for gas. Imagine the price of food, already rising rapidly, shooting up 10 percent or more in just a couple weeks. When Congress introduces new taxes, you had better bet it's us, the American middle class, the small business owners, and young families struggling to make ends meet, who will pay the price.

Instead of picking winners and losers, Congress should focus on lowering rates for everyone, eliminating corporate loopholes, and simplifying the tax code for both families and businesses. This kind of commonsense tax reform enjoys massive support from members of every party, race, creed, color of America.

The American people need a consistent, stable economy where they can thrive by buying the goods they need while saving money for a rainy day. However, the Border Adjustment Tax is just another tax on middle- and low-income families with a fancy name.

Republicans from Texas should be leading the fight for tax reform and opposing the new American Middle-Class Consumer Tax. This is exactly what the American people elected President Trump and a Republican Congress to do last November. Congress has failed on repealing ObamaCare and better not fail us on tax reform ... and instead add another new tax!

PART 4
Liberal Politics
and the Media

Lies and Liberal Politics

Liberal Media News or Propaganda

The facts never seem to deter liberals. When they want to push a message, liberal politicians and their allies in the media do not seem to care about the truth.

The latest example is the claim that Republican presidential nominee Mitt Romney is responsible for the death of an employee at a steel plant because Bain Capital purchased and closed the factory. The inference is that the employee, Joe Soptic, lost his job and his health care. And thus his ill wife died, and of course it's all Romney's fault.

The facts are that Romney stopped working for Bain in 1999. The plant closed in 2001, and the man's wife died in 2006. Soptic admitted to CNN on Tuesday, August 7, that the family in fact had health insurance at the time of his wife's death. However, liberals, including the media, won't admit or hear the facts and still blame Romney.

Last week, Senate Majority Leader Harry Reid (D-Nevada) accused Romney of being a tax cheat. Not only has Reid pushed this lie; the Obama White House and campaign have also asked Romney to release his taxes. Again the facts are that Romney has always paid his taxes in a timely and honest manner, and he has never had any problems with the IRS and/or any state taxing agency. Instead of Romney's taxes, we should all ask for Obama to release his college records, which have been sealed.

Big lies are not limited to the national political stage. Democrat US Congressmen Henry Cuellar, Charlie Gonzalez, Ruben Hinojosa, and Lloyd Doggett from Texas have all said the Tea Party is at fault for a national credit rating downgrade. These liberal congressmen ignored Standard and Poor's assertion that "the debt and spending" have to be brought under control.

It is difficult to understand how excessive federal spending, which began several decades ago, is the Tea Party's fault since the primary goal of the Tea Party is to cut government spending.

Liberal Texas state legislators have pushed many other lies on the public. They say the voter ID law is discriminatory and minority congressional districts are necessary for minorities to be elected. However, Ted Cruz and Congressman Francisco "Quico" Canseco have proven that minorities can be elected with rarely mentioning their ethnicity.

Ralph Waldo Emerson once said, "Every violation of truth is not only a sort of suicide in the liar, but is a stab at the health of human society." There is an illness among liberals since they prefer to accept fiction over fact.

Many voters accept these lies because it is either convenient or they are uninformed. In either case, voters must find and elect honest persons to local, state, and federal government, or American society cannot long endure.

Spanish-Language Media: Dividing America and Segregating Hispanics

Media Bias and Spanish-Language Media

In the next few weeks, TV network Univision will host a presidential debate for Obama and Romney, while the local Univision station in San Antonio will host a debate for US Congressman Quico Canseco (Texas-23) and challenger Pete Gallego. Both debates will be in Spanish for Spanish-speaking audiences.

In today's America where being politically correct is important, hardly anyone blinks at political debates in Spanish. However, we must ask if Spanish-language media, particularly television and radio, are dividing America and segregating Hispanics.

First, Univision and Telemundo are obsessed with the immigration issue. Why? Because they are playing to their Spanish-speaking market. Imagine what would happen to Spanish-language TV if their market started learning English. Thus, it is important that they dramatize the issue of immigration to their audience. They need to keep Spanish-speaking immigrants coming to the United States, even if illegally, to replenish their audience.

Second, their TV reporters and radio commentators are overwhelmingly liberal, and Hispanics are routinely portrayed as victims of American society. When the state voter ID law was debated, a Univision reporter in Austin claimed there were never any examples of voter fraud in Texas history. Telemundo's national anchor Jose Diaz-Balart has attacked the Tea Party as racist without ever interviewing a Tea Party leader. Both networks always refer to the conservative position on illegal immigration as "anti-immigrant."

The problem is that Spanish-language media is influencing the future of America by dividing the nation and segregating Hispanics. Univision and Telemundo are more popular than ABC, NBC, and CBS. Yet while there are conservative watchdog groups that monitor the mainstream media, no one is monitoring Spanish-language media.

Given this media influence, we should ask: when will Hispanics assimilate into American society? Language is a unifying factor for our nation. However, because language is primary to Spanish-speaking media, they support and defend any politician who plays to their agenda—that is, maintaining a Spanish-speaking market.

The fact is that Spanish-language media is isolating a large population in America, and it is helping to create two different societies. In order to prevent this division, three things must happen:

1. We need Spanish-speaking conservatives to appear and comment on Spanish-language news reports and programs on a regular basis. Conservatives should have a Spanish-speaking Rush Limbaugh to get the conservative message into the Spanish-speaking community, particularly in Texas.
2. Conservatives must promote English as the first language of the nation, and Spanish-language media should promote English to their audience.
3. Conservatives must monitor national and local Spanish-speaking media and hold them responsible for fairness in reporting. They must not be allowed to promote a liberal agenda.

The English language is a unifying factor for our nation, and it is time for Spanish-language media to celebrate, encourage, and embrace it. We cannot have two societies separated by language.

Local Media Bias

Media Bias

While national political talk shows are buzzing about moderator Candy Crowley's behavior during the recent presidential debate, we don't have to look far in south Texas to see examples of that type of journalistic bias. Crowley clearly jumped to President Obama's defense when Mitt Romney pressed Obama on the Libyan terrorist attacks. She tried to explain herself after the debate, but her bias and partisanship had been exposed.

Unfortunately we have examples of such bias journalism in south Texas. Recently, a local reporter in San Antonio was going to do a hit piece about a conservative group based on his legal interpretation of PAC laws. The reporter was defending liberal Mayor Julian Castro's policies. Although the reporter is not an attorney and did not have a full understanding of the law, he was ready to attack the conservative group. Luckily, after speaking to an attorney who is a PAC expert, the reporter decided to seek the advice of a law professor before writing the story. It is amazing that he was going to do a critical story based on his legal assumptions and not legal knowledge.

There are newspaper editors and reporters in south Texas who refuse to recognize or even speak to conservatives. The owner/editor of one Valley newspaper told me he would not speak to Tea Party supporters because he felt they were "radicals and Neanderthals." With that kind of attitude, how could local conservatives expect fair and balanced coverage?

George H. Rodriguez

There are also small newspapers that see themselves as local versions of the *New York Times* or *Washington Post*. They are too sophisticated for the local conservatives and either ignore or contradict them without reason.

However, there are those newspapers that are fair, such as the *Wilson County News* in Floresville, Texas. *WCN* has done a great job of reporting on a grassroots rebellion against the local Hispanic Democratic establishment that has done everything from alleged racism to enlist the support from US Congressman Henry Cuellar and the National Association of Latino Elected Officials (NALEO) to counter the challenge to his liberal establishment. However, WCN has not backed off, and neither have the local grassroots citizens and their allies. The stories have always been fair and balanced, as the truth has been told.

The *Seguin Gazette* is another great example of a balanced newspaper. The *Gazette* runs a weekly side-by-side, liberal versus conservative editorial opinion pieces. The dueling editorials give the public a fair and balanced view on the issues.

Unfortunately many reporters and editors have decided to support popular trends rather than report on the facts. It may be difficult for a reporter to cover a story in an unbiased manner, but that is his or her role.

The challenge to editors is to have a balance of opinions. There is no room for bias in the media, whether it is a large market like New York or a small market like Val Verde County, Texas.

Parents/Families versus the Media and Obama

Media Bias and Redefining Families

This past week, Melissa Harris-Perry of MSNBC said, "We have to break through our kind of private idea that kids belong to their parents or kids belong to their families and recognize that kids belong to whole communities. Once it's everyone's responsibility and not just the household's, then we start making better investments."

The collective approach to education is not new to people who want to use government to reshape society. The communists used it in Soviet Russia, and the Nazis used it in Germany. In the United States, liberals have accelerated their efforts to expand the influence of government on children while lessening that of parents since Hillary Clinton wrote her book in 1996, *It Takes a Village*.

During this state legislative session in Austin, state lawmakers have wrestled with C-SCOPE and pre-K legislation along with liberal demands to give more funding to public schools.

CSCOPE, a system used by public schools, has received many complaints from faculty and parents because they were not permitted to review lesson plans. Others complained about the lack of oversight from the State Board of Education and for lessons that undermined conservative values for the sake of political correctness.

Then there is the push for prekindergarten (pre-K), which is supposed to place four-year-olds in classroom and learning environments.

President Obama announced in his 2014 budget that preschool for all low- and moderate-income four-year-olds would be funded by a new federal-state partnership. In Texas, State Representative Mike Villarreal (D-Dist.123 / San Antonio) has introduced legislation for a statewide pre-K program.

However, the clear issue is whether the state or family/parent can best socialize a child. Diana Baumrind, a psychologist at the University of California, Berkeley, found that the best parent is one who is involved and responsive, who sets high expectations but respects his or her child's autonomy. These parents raise children who do better academically, psychologically, and socially. Another psychologist, Carol Dweck at Stanford University, found that involved parents raised more successful children because there was a sense of belonging.

Yet another clinician, Madeline Levine, wrote in the *New York Times* in August 2012 that one of the most important things that a parent can do is to present children with a version of adult life that is appealing and worth striving for.

But in an Orwellian ideal that is typical of authoritarian societies, liberals want the government to replace the family's influence on children. Liberals justify this approach because of working mothers and because the traditional family broke down. Never mind that the government's social welfare programs helped break the traditional family. Liberals still justified the government stepping in to fill the role of parents and family.

The bottom line is that liberals believe in the collective and that parents are not capable because they might teach the child a non–politically correct lesson of individualism and Judeo-Christian morals. In a very rare and honest moment, Melissa Harris-Perry of MSNBC exposed the liberals' true education agenda. If liberals are to succeed in changing America, the children are the key.

Does the Constitution Still Protect Me under Obama?

Media and Free Speech

It appears that I must be "an enemy of the state," as defined by the Obama administration. As the former president of the San Antonio Tea Party, the current president of a 501c4 nonprofit group, and a conservative opinion writer and blogger, I must be on their watch list.

I was president of the San Antonio Tea Party when we received a lengthy questionnaire from the now famous Cincinnati IRS office. However, the cover letter came from Ogden, Utah. The recent congressional hearings have shown that a counselor in President Obama's office was aware of the overreaching behavior.

During the House Committee hearing on Wednesday, May 22, former IRS Commissioner Doug Shulman said he would not take "personal responsibility" for the creation of a list that was used to subject Tea Party and other groups to excessive scrutiny. And he provided few new explanations for why he did not notify Congress about the program despite learning about it in May 2012.

The IRS's behavior indeed had a chilling effect on many Tea Party participants who were fearful of IRS audits or punitive actions. Some leaders of the San Antonio Tea Party were almost paralyzed with fear of the IRS. In that vein, the IRS minimized, by intent or not, conservative grassroots participation during the 2012 election season.

I must ask myself if I am under further scrutiny since I am president of the South Texas Alliance for Progress, a conservative nonprofit group that informs and educates voters about local issues. I am also a conservative opinion blogger and writer, and I have watched with interest how the Justice Department has targeted reporters as coconspirators for doing their job.

Court documents recently revealed that the Justice Department had seized the records of several Fox News phone lines as part of a leak investigation, and according to one source, they even matched the home phone number of a reporter's parents. There was also a court-approved search warrant for Fox News correspondent James Rosen's personal emails. In the affidavit seeking that warrant, an FBI agent called Rosen a likely criminal coconspirator, citing a wartime law called the Espionage Act.

Besides the Fox News reporter's records, the Justice Department also issued a subpoena for the AP phone records of five reporters' cell phones, three home phones, and two fax lines. David Schulz, the chief lawyer for the AP, said the subpoenas also covered the records for twenty-one phone lines, including a dead phone line at an office in Washington. The subpoenas also covered the phone lines at four other offices where about a hundred reporters worked. Through all of this and the Benghazi cover-up too, President Obama denies any knowledge and thus responsibility for his administration's actions.

As an outspoken conservative who expresses his opinions regularly on Facebook, in emails, on the phone, in public, and in editorial columns and who has been and is currently president of a conservative organization, I must ask myself if I am still protected by the US Constitution under this current president.

Should the Constitution Protect Me, a Blogger?

Free Speech

In the latest attempt to revise the US Constitution, liberal Illinois senator Dick Durbin questioned if the US Constitution should protect bloggers. Durbin told Chris Wallace of Fox News that he doubted whether bloggers, or "someone who is Tweeting," should be given media shield rights. "Here is the bottom line," he said, "the media shield law, which I am prepared to support still leaves an unanswered question, which I have raised many times: What is a journalist today in 2013? We know it's someone that works for Fox or AP, but does it include a blogger? Does it include someone who is tweeting? Are these people journalists and entitled to constitutional protection?"

Obviously Durbin doesn't believe the First Amendment protection of free speech includes a person speaking via a blog, a tweet, or email. In typical liberal fashion, Durbin feels we need to review "twenty-first-century questions about a provision in our Constitution that was written over two hundred years ago."

To be sure, the First Amendments states, "Congress shall make no law respecting an establishment of religion, or prohibiting the free exercise thereof; or abridging the freedom of speech, or of the press; or the right of the people peaceably to assemble, and to petition the Government for a redress of grievances."

Like it or not, liberals like Senator Durbin should understand that all Americans are protected by the Constitution under the First Amendment, not just journalists. As such, I have the same right to freedom of speech as a blogger and part-time opinion writer as anyone at the *New York Times* or *Washington Post*. However, it's a bit scary to realize that a United States senator doesn't believe the First Amendment applies equally to all Americans.

At the heart of Durbin's position, as well as many other liberals, is the idea that the Constitution is outdated and must be changed. Durbin does not believe that truths are constant and eternal, such as the fact that individual freedoms must be protected from governments. In fact, this whole issue and discussion is the result of the government through Eric Holder and the Justice Department monitoring journalists.

The last few weeks, we have seen the Obama administration use the IRS to attempt to suppress conservative political groups and their right of free speech because they disagreed with his politics. They monitored journalists at Fox News and CBS who were doing their job in investigative reporting. It is sad to see that we have such insecure leaders who feel they have to bend the law to silence their opponents. This is what happens when people fear the First Amendment.

The First Amendment protects all Americans in their right to debate and disagree with the government, provided they do not advocate violence. While nonprofessional citizen journalists who use tweets and blogs are new forms of information decimation, it is free speech nonetheless, and they are protected.

As for the question of "Should the Constitution protect me?" the answer should be an emphatic yes!

June 6, 2013

Silence of the Liberals

Media and Liberal Politics

Liberal US Congressmen Pete Gallego, Joaquin Castro, Lloyd Doggett, and Henry Cuellar have been very silent about the recent Obama administration scandals, and the media doesn't seem to mind.

For example, the IRS has been targeting Tea Party groups, antiabortion, and other conservative groups by holding up their applications for tax exemptions, harassing them with questions, and leaking their donor lists to political opponents. However, all four liberal south Texas congressmen (Gallego, Castro, Doggett, and Cuellar) have yet to make a comment or utter a peep about the issue. Apparently they ignore the fact that they have Tea Party members in their districts.

These same congressmen have also been silent regarding the Justice Department's subpoena of news media records, and Attorney General Eric Holder's apparent misleading testimony to Congress. Whereas some congressmen are demanding answers and accountability from Holder, these four haven't said anything.

There is also the latest black eye for the IRS where the agency provided Congress a video of the IRS workers practicing their dance moves. Again there is only silence from the Fab Four. This comes after two previous videos that show agency workers in a parody of the *Star Trek* and *Gilligan's Island* TV shows. There was no comment about those two videos either.

As for the Benghazi attack the Fab Four congressmen have not said anything about what many now openly describe as a full-blown cover-up related to the terrorist attack on September 11, 2012. What we have here is the death of four brave Americans and a subsequent cover-up for the purposes of maintaining political power. And these four congressmen say nothing. Based on their silence, we can only conclude that they are either not interested in doing their job for the people they represent, or they are playing politics by being silent.

Gallego, Castro, Doggett, and Cuellar have been quick to defend the Obama administration on other issues. They support amnesty for eleven million illegal aliens, and they don't believe there is a spending problem that has led America to a $16 trillion deficit. Cuellar went so far as to blame the Tea Party for the downgrade in the nation's credit rating last year.

What is apparent is that all four congressmen do not represent conservative constituents in their districts. They support liberal issues, carry the line for the Democratic Party, and defend the Obama administration's policies, but what about finding out the truth on these scandals and bringing about a just resolution? What about upholding and defending the Constitution of the United States?

The voters and citizens in their districts should hold them accountable. Either they represent all of the citizens in their district or only certain ones. Either they uphold the Constitution or they are only interested in defending their party.

There are sins of commission, such as Eric Holder lying to Congress about his knowledge of investigating reporters, and sins of omission such as these four congressmen and their lack of interest in cleaning up the scandalous behavior of Obama administration officials.

Gallego, Castro, Doggett, and Cuellar need to stop playing politics and do their job in representing all of their constituents because their silence is deafening ... and revealing.

Cyber Walls That Protect or Imprison

Media and Privacy

Are the walls of a fortress meant to protect or imprison? A nation's walls, real or cyber, are meant to protect its citizens and boundaries from foreign incursion. However, those same defenses can be turned into the imprisonment of its citizens such as the Berlin Wall and the old Iron Curtain.

The Great Wall of China was built to protect China, but more specifically it was to protect the Chinese emperor from Mongol invaders. On the other hand, the Chinese slave laborers who built the wall probably viewed the project more as a prison, not as a protector.

Likewise, today, the Obama government is gathering and mining information from internet systems under the pretext of protecting the nation and its citizens. The information gathering has been justified to thwart foreign terrorist attacks. But can we trust this government—or any government—to use this information to protect its citizens and not eventually imprison them?

The goal of Obama and his supporters from the beginning has been to fundamentally change America. They have worked around Congress and the Constitution by using executive orders to mandate rules and regulations when they could not pass laws through Congress. They have been less than truthful in matters such as the Benghazi attack and with the IRS scandal. They have released dangerous illegal aliens from

US detention centers but halted hot meals for soldiers in Afghanistan in the name of sequester. They have undermined parents by providing birth control to girls under the age of sixteen without their permission or knowledge. They have supported same-sex marriage by pushing for the reversal of laws that were legally and lawfully passed by a majority of voters such as Proposition 8 in California. Given this track record, should we not worry if the federal government's wall of protection could become a prison for its citizens?

When the government begins to access phone records, information on our purchasing habits, and the items we purchased and they hold up the IRS applications of groups they disagree with, should we, particularly constitutional conservatives, not worry?

President Reagan used to quote the Russian proverb of "trust but verify" regarding the negotiations with the Soviets. Unfortunately at this time in our nation's history, we cannot trust or verify.

America is great because of the constitutional freedoms it gives us as citizens. If those constitutional freedoms and guarantees go away, national protection becomes national imprisonment. A government "of the people, by the people, and for the people" becomes a government for itself.

I believe gathering information about foreign nationals is a matter of national security and necessity. However, it is also my opinion the Obama administration does not respect the US Constitution, which protects me, and since I cannot trust or verify why, how, and who will see or use my personal information, I do not want to add another brick to a wall that may become my prison.

Social Media as Tool for Liberty and Independence

Media

Less than three weeks after grassroots conservative activists won a big victory in the Texas GOP state convention by strengthening the Republican platform on immigration, activists have now forced the state government to address the current immigration crisis on the Texas-Mexico border. They did this by using their new tool, social media and personal communication devices.

For several weeks, an ever-increasing number of illegal aliens have been entering the United States with little to no support or response from President Obama and state-elected Democrats. Over 160,000 illegal aliens have been caught and detained in the south Texas sector alone, including 60,000 minors, just since October 2013.

As a result of this invasion, a group of grassroots activist Texans went on Facebook and began to organize a petition to ask Texas Governor Rick Perry to call a special session of the state legislature to deal with this crisis. The group was led by Ms. Terri Hill, a housewife from Longview, who started a movement on Facebook that then spread to other social media.

Within days of the start of the petition, the state GOP leaders reacted. On Wednesday, June 18, they authorized the Texas Department of Public Safety to spend about $1.3 million per week to fund operations to fight the surge of illegal immigration along the Texas-Mexico border.

Governor Perry, Lieutenant Governor David Dewhurst, and House Speaker Joe Straus issued a joint statement saying that the "law enforcement surge operations" comes as the result of "the absence of adequate resources to secure the border." Additionally, Texas attorney general Greg Abbott asked the US Homeland Security Department for $30 million so Texas could send more state troopers to the border.

All of this action, or reaction, happened because one housewife used social media to rally her fellow grassroots patriots, who responded with their smart phones, laptops, desktops, and other personal devices for social communication.

In Texas and across the nation, we have seen the conservative grassroots movement organize itself using social media. There are an increasing number of alternative news and information sources on social, such as Breitbart, and internet podcast shows, such as RagingElephantsRadio.com.

All of this is reaction to two main issues:

1. There is a lack of confidence in the mainstream media, which has repeatedly shown its liberal bias.
2. It gives political independence to the grassroots common folks who can speak and organize without depending on local, state, or national political leaders or organizations.

Last year, the mainstream media applauded and marveled at the use of social media during the Arab Spring, but conversely they have ignored the Tea Party Spring in our country. The examples of this movement are clear: the aforementioned defeat of the Texas Solution at the state GOP convention; the defeat of Congressman Eric Cantor in Virginia; and the demand that the state government do what the federal government is not doing.

It's a different ballgame, folks. Whereas the minutemen of old grabbed their muskets to fight for freedom and liberty in their day, today's patriots are grabbing their personal communications devices and communicating via social media.

November 23, 2016

Media Fears and Trump's Administration

Media Bias

The mainstream media is worried about the possible ramifications of a problem they created. CNN's British-Iranian talk show host, Christiane Amanpour, is worried that there will be government censorship under Trump. No, Ms. Amanpour. That might be how they do it in other countries, but in the United States, we let the free market rule. In the privacy of our homes and cars, we still can and will choose what media sources we watch or hear.

Mainstream media personalities like Amanpour, particularly those with a globalist view, still don't understand the damage they did to themselves in this past election campaign. They don't understand the majority of Americans have recognized their smug, arrogant, elitist bias, and the government (Trump) doesn't have to censor them. The average American will censor them by turning them off or changing the channel. It is called freedom.

Furthermore, the mainstream media is upset at the competition from alternative media sources of news and information, or alt media. The mainstream folks hate competition, and CNN has gone so far as warning their viewers that independent outlets are biased and misleading. That's laughable irony considering WikiLeaks exposed CNN as a little more than propaganda mouthpiece for Hillary and Democrats and has declared war on alternative media in an article by

Brian Stelter. If anyone wants censorship, it's the mainstream media because they don't like competition.

Whether it is a national mainstream media source like the *Washington Post, New York Times, LA Times*, CNN, ABC News, CBS News, NBC News, Univision, or Telemundo, they are all having a difficult time coping with or accepting the fact that most Texans and Americans view them with deep skepticism or outright reject them. They caused the problem but refuse to accept the responsibility.

In every popular revolution, the first thing the establishment rulers try to do is discredit the opposition and prevent them from communicating and disseminating information. Let's remember the Obama administration has supported Net Neutrality, which the government would regulate in the name of fairness. And remember how fair they have been.

Also remember how Obama handed over control of the internet in October 2016 to ICANN, a group that includes the 108 members of the UN, including Russia, China, Iran, and Saudi Arabia. We all know how friendly those countries are to First Amendment rights.

It is obvious the mainstream media in the United States will not ever be fair and balanced. They will always report news and information from their liberal/progressive/globalist point of view. The best hope for Texans and all Americans is to continue to create and develop alternative media sources for international and national reports, but also for regional and local reports.

Tyrants are their own worst enemies. That goes for the mainstream media. Unlike liberal/progressives, we don't need the government to protect us. Free-thinking Texans and Americans will censor the biased mainstream media by simply changing the channel.

The Media Meltdown Continues over the Trump Election, Even on the Local Level

Media Bias

The local and national liberal/leftist mainstream media is doing a great job of misleading and dividing the public over the Trump temporary immigration ban by calling it discriminatory. Saul Alinsky, Lenin, Fidel Castro, Goebbels, and Mao would be proud of them.

Personally, I am curious as to where these reporters and protesters were when the Obama IRS targeted me for simply being a Tea Party leader? Where were they when veterans in Texas and elsewhere were receiving poor or no health care from the VA? Where were they when the DNC and Hillary supporters clearly stacked the primary election against Bernie Sanders? Where were they when Planned Parenthood was caught red-handed selling baby body parts?

It has become very obvious that the media is heavily responsible for undermining the Constitution, law and order, and Christian values in American today. They are little more than propagandist agitators that inspire emotional responses from the public rather than inform with logic and facts.

Grassroots citizens must fight back against the media by using social media and truth. This is particularly important with local media that simply repeats the national media's liberal message. They rarely bother to find counterresponses to the leftist new messages.

Since the 1965 War on Poverty and the civil rights movement, the mainstream media has helped politicians to manipulate citizens with biased, one-sided liberal news reporting.

State and local media are critical because that's where the power of the people starts. "All politics is local," and informing and educating voters/citizens starts at the local level. Fair, unemotional, and balanced reporting is important so people can make rational, logical, and fact-based decisions about their national, state, and local politics and economy.

It appears the Trump administration is going to have a rough relationship with the national media, and the state and local media will just repeat their comments. That could bode badly for the citizens and voters who want to be informed.

An objective and unbiased media is important, particularly at the state and local level because the defense of personal freedom and liberty, along with controlling the power of local and state government, starts in your back at the voting booth.

Local Elections and Social Media

Media Bias

Candidates and issues need exposure and publicity for citizens and voters to hear and see them, and exposure and publicity costs money, especially for first-time candidates. But in today's world of social media, exposure and publicity can sometimes be had cheaply and easily.

Traditional campaigns use workers, flyers, TV/radio ads, billboards, and large venues for rallies. All of that costs money. Also the media can be biased against lesser-known or first-time candidates by ignoring them in favor of incumbents or personalities or by digging up old dirt that might have been resolved long ago.

Grassroots candidates, especially first-time candidates, are usually not well known and have little money. If they are not well known, it is difficult to get contributions and purchase publicity. The lack of exposure becomes a big political disadvantage to challengers.

However, the game can change dramatically with social media. Social media has been called "the people's media" because people control what they write and read. Facebook, Twitter, email, and other forms of social media can send out information in moments and challenge incumbents and deep-pocket, establishment candidates.

Social media can provide exposure for the candidates and their messages. There are many bloggers and podcasters with large social media followings and audiences. Citizens and voters can learn about candidates and their positions via social media, and they can even interact and ask questions. Think about how accessible the establishment or incumbent candidate is to voters.

Second, the media will always cover incumbent and popular candidates, especially if they have the money to buy publicity, but they will ignore lesser-known candidates. The media can also give negative press to the lesser-known candidates, which can end their campaigns or political aspirations. The media will literally create its own buzz and exposure at the expense of the lesser-known, possibly better-qualified candidates.

Social media bloggers/podcasters can help lesser-known candidates with exposure, and they can also help them counter the media's biased reporting and editorial attacks. The establishment media will always claim impartiality, but the facts in past campaigns show otherwise. Independent bloggers/podcasters can help a lesser-known candidate set the record straight.

Finally social media is inexpensive compared to flyers, billboards, campaign workers, TV/radio ads, and large venues. Candidates can control their own campaign messages and reach a large number of voters and citizens through social media without much money.

Social media bloggers/podcasters can provide the exposure and publicity that lesser-known or first-time candidates need, and they can do it cheaply. Obviously it is not the only tool for a campaign, but it can be a very big one.

The grassroots movement needs social media to help its candidates campaign against local, state, and national establishments by informing and educating the citizens and voters. It is populist free press versus big establishment press. We should remember that the defense of freedom and liberty starts locally in our backyard and we must stay informed.

San Antonio Express-News Tells Taxpayers/Citizens to "Deal with It"

Media Bias and Local Tyranny

In an extraordinary show of arrogance, the liberal *San Antonio Express-News* ran an editorial on Wednesday, February 15, with a headline that read, "Toll roads are necessary; deal with it." The title seemed to tell the public, "Shut up, stop opposing toll roads, and get in line."

The *San Antonio Express-News* is the speakerphone for the San Antonio / Bexar County establishment, which includes big business, politicians, and the local government bureaucracy. This establishment usually pursues its own agenda over the will of the people and at taxpayer expense.

The editorial says the "state lawmakers have shown zero interest in raising the gas tax, which is exactly why toll roads need to be on the table." Apparently they can't understand why state legislators would listen to voters who don't want toll roads and don't want taxes raised. Rather than advocate for raising taxes, why not suggest tax revenues be redirected? Better yet, why not tell the elected officials and establishment to "deal with it" because citizens don't want toll roads.

It also says, "The 1604 (road) project is expected to cost $882 million, but tolls would reduce that cost to taxpayers to $326 million," but the tolls add $556 million to lower the cost. However, local conservative activist Stanley Mitchell and Harvard-educated MBA, points out that establishment leaders, Bexar County judge Nelson Wolff and former

VIA CEO Henry Munoz, moved some VIA road improvement funds four years ago that were designated for roads to the streetcar project. That money transfer resulted in a $460 million loss when a voters petition terminated the streetcar project. Why should taxpayers pay for a boondoggle the establishment pursued?

The op-ed also says the state gas tax hasn't been raised since 1991 when it went to 20 cents a gallon and the minimum wage was $4.25 an hour. It suggests it should be raised because of inflation and population increase. Taxpayers should want more taxation?

The editorial concludes by saying, "The goal here is to keep people moving. Toll roads help make that happen. We only slow ourselves down when we frame the issue any other way."

Strangling traffic by closing lanes and limiting private transportation appears to be meant to frustrate commuters out of the cars. The establishment is also banking on that frustration turning into a willingness to pay higher taxes for mass transportation projects.

The *San Antonio Express-News* will continue to beat the drum for toll roads. It is the loudest, most liberal voice in south Texas, and the banner says it all. "Toll roads are necessary; deal with it." It shows the disrespect they and the establishment have toward the opinions of citizens and voters who do not support their agenda.

Perhaps it's time to remind the *San Antonio Express-News* and the Bexar County / San Antonio establishment that citizens and voters don't want toll roads and they should "deal with it."

The Biased National and Local Media

Media Bias

President Trump gave a major dustup to the national mainstream media yesterday, Thursday, February 16, in Washington, DC, and many people felt it was a long time coming and applauded it. However, the state and local press copies the national media because many of the reporters want to be promoted to the national stage. Consequentially state/local media often imitate the national press in their biased reporting of issues.

For example, when was the last time the San Antonio press did a hard investigative report of city hall and downtown development? When was the last time the Dallas press did a thorough analysis of the Dallas County commissioners court and their agenda? When was the last time the *Houston Chronicle* questioned the voter registration roles in Harris County? When was the last time the *Austin Statesman* or any news outlet did an investigation regarding donations to state and local politicians and what those donors got in return? When was the last time they connected the dots for the citizens and voters?

State and local media should not reflect the news bias of their national counterparts. They view and report news in a leftist, politically correct, establishment-bias manner. For example, the phrase "illegal alien" has been erased completely from the news. They routinely run antifracking reports on front pages or Sunday editions.

Another great example was in 2013 when pro-abortion supporters responded to pro-life supporters praying at the state capitol with chants of "Hail Satan." The mainstream media did not report that scene at all. Only conservative news outlets, the *Blaze* and *Red State*, reported it.

The state and local mainstream media has become a true advocate for liberal policies while ignoring the will of the people. Another classic example was the February 15 *San Antonio Express-News* editorial that was entitled "Toll roads are necessary; deal with it." The *San Antonio Express* editorial board ignored that a majority of Texas voters have opposed toll roads and literally told citizens their opinions on public policy don't matter. Such is the arrogance of state and local media.

While some people say there are conservative radio programs that can balance the liberal media, the fact is that these conservative programs deal with national issues and rarely focus on politics at the state capitol, the county courthouse, or city hall.

After a nasty presidential campaign where evidence of media and Democratic Party collusion was discovered several times, the grassroots voters and citizens should be very suspicious of the national mainstream media. But the state and local media, particularly the Spanish-language media, are reporting the news in a biased manner, and citizens and voters should wake up to that fact. They ignore the grassroots point of view while they promote the leftist and/or establishment agenda.

There is a real need for conservative news analysis and commentaries to counter the powerful and large mainstream media. The defense of freedom and liberty starts in our backyard, and we cannot defend it if we fail to understand or recognize the tyranny.

Jorge Ramos Says, "This Is Our Country"

Immigration and Spanish-Language Media

Jorge Ramos continued to sound anti-American when he repeated some provocative comments on Tucker Carlson's show on March 8 that he originally made in late February. He again stated, "This is not a white country. This is not their country. It is ours." Who is "ours," and is he using his Spanish-language media platform to divide American society?

Ramos's comment should wake up all red-blooded American citizens because it was racist and anti-American. It is the very same message that Univision, Telemundo, and other Spanish-language media outlets promote directly and indirectly, actively and passively, on a daily basis.

The message is about the justified conquest of America by people of color in response to (revenge for) the colonization of the Third World. America is the big target because it is considered the worst offender, the "great Satan." Mexico has been angry at the United States since 1836 and 1848 when they lost Texas and the Southwest respectively. And never mind that the United States paid Mexico $15 million even though they'd won the war.

When Ramos speaks about immigration, he is not referring to legal or controlled immigration. He's talking about all-out, open-border immigration, including illegal aliens. Rarely does he or anyone in Spanish-language news differentiate between illegal and legal immigration.

Ramos also used the race card. He said whites are afraid of losing the country and that border and immigration controls are about race, not national security or sovereignty.

But has Ramos looked in the mirror? He is white. In fact, all the Mexican media is filled with blonds and blue-eyed people, along with non-Mexican, Indian-looking people. Ramos yells racism because he ignores that it exists in Latino culture.

Ramos ignores how Mexicans use the word *indio* with all the negative connotations of the N-word in English. People who are *prietos*, or dark skinned, are discriminated against politically, economically, and socially, even within families sometimes.

Mexican society and other Latino nations are filled with racism and racist stereotypes, and they have dishonest government leaders who deny this fact. Those attitudes are sometimes even found among Latinos in the United States.

Ramos tried to explain and soften his comments on Fox News, but he still sounds like the pot calling the kettle racist. He sounded more like a subversive element who uses the media for his platform to criticize and divide American society and undermine the legal system by defending illegal aliens who broke the law. His comments also frighten and mislead Spanish-speaking people who hear him.

Intentionally or not, Spanish-language media is segregating Latinos and subverting America's future by encouraging cultural and linguistic separatism rather than assimilation.

It is truly ironic that Ramos is excited about the day when whites will become a minority since he is a green-eyed white male himself. It appears Jorge Ramos is not an American who supports the Constitution and law and order but a racist immigrant who is antagonistic toward American society and history.

August 23, 2017

What Can Conservatives Do about Fake News?

Politics and the Media

We are witnessing another example of fake news trying to manipulate society and politics in the wake of President Trump's speech in Phoenix last night. The liberal CNN called Trump's speech "scary," while the liberal *San Antonio Express-News* called it "a rant" on its lead banner.

National and local fake news / mainstream media is showing its partisan leftist face, again, with its criticism of the Phoenix Trump speech. They claim that Trump is creating a new civil war, but in reality they are the ones alienating most Americans. CNN's Don Lemon said Trump is "unhinged" and claimed he lied. Former national intelligence director James Clapper claimed Trump was divisive and not mentally competent. Several minority commentators used the race card in their criticism.

But it's all one-sided criticism. For example, CNN and other news media never criticized former president Obama when he hosted Black Lives Matter at the White House.

So what can average Americans do about national and local fake news, other than ignore it and not watch or read it? We should all understand that whether it's national CNN or MSNBC or the local *San Antonio Express-News*, it is ads, not subscribers, that keep fake news afloat. Businesses that advertise in fake news pay their bills and salaries.

Furthermore, businesses are much more afraid of the leftist PC police, of being called racist, sexist, homophobic, and anti-immigrant. The left has intimidated businesses with political correctness.

Businesses could buy ads on conservative websites, podcasts, radio, TV programs, and newsletters. However, businesses that buy ads on liberal fake news media could also support conservative news. But they're too afraid of the PC police.

Leftist/liberal fake news is a national security problem, and businesses that advertise with fake news outlets are supporting them and their anti-American, anti-Constitution, anti-freedom-and-liberty agenda. Has the idea of being fair and balanced with their ad money become too fearful for businesses? Are they willing to let the left silence conservative opinions too?

Perhaps we should ask businesses that advertise in fake news outlets if they are anti-American, anti-Constitution, anti-personal-freedom-and-liberty.

Printed in the United States
By Bookmasters